BROKEN MARY

MARY

A JOURNEY OF HOPE

KEVIN MATTHEWS

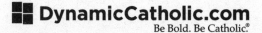

DynamicCatholic.com

Be Bold. Be Catholic.®

Cover design: Jessie Sayward Bright

ISBN: 978-1-942611-68-4 (hardcover)
ISBN: 978-1-942611-69-1 (softcover)

Library of Congress Cataloging-in-Publication Data
Names: Matthews, Kevin (Radio personality), author.
Title: Broken Mary : a journey of hope /
Kevin Matthews.
Description: North Palm Beach, FL : Beacon Pub., 2016.
Identifiers: LCCN 2016015237 (print) | LCCN 2016016000
(ebook) | ISBN 9781942611684 (hardcover) |
ISBN 9781942611691 (softcover) | ISBN 9781942611707
(ebook)
Subjects: LCSH: Fatima, Our Lady of. | Mary, Blessed Virgin,
Saint--Apparitions and miracles. | Matthews, Kevin (Radio
personality | Radio personalities--Illinois--Chicago--Biography.
| Multiple sclerosis--Patients--Religious life.
Classification: LCC BT660.F3 M38 2016 (print) | LCC BT660.
F3 (ebook) | DDC
282.092 [B] --dc23
LC record available at https://lccn.loc.gov/2016015237

Dynamic Catholic® and Be Bold. Be Catholic.® and The Best Version of Yourself®
are registered trademarks of The Dynamic Catholic Institute.

For more information on this title or other books and CDs available through the
Dynamic Catholic Book Program, please visit www.DynamicCatholic.com.

The Dynamic Catholic Institute
5081 Olympic Blvd • Erlanger • Kentucky • 41018
Phone: 1–859–980–7900
Email: info@DynamicCatholic.com

Printed in the United States of America

[1]

This book is for my wife, Debra, who has a tender heart, a most infectious laugh, and is the beautiful mother of the two treasures of my life.

Contents

PART II
Broken Mary

Foreword

A few years ago, when I was researching contemporary radio for a talk I was to give at my university, I happened upon *The Morning Show* on WLAV-FM (96.9), Grand Rapids, Michigan. The radio man, Kevin Matthews, was running through the events of the previous evening, commenting on some of the particulars as he went. Pretty soon he was interrupted by his ill-mannered sports reporter, Jim Shorts, who wanted to complain about the Tigers' performance. Kevin was patient; Jim was annoyed. Kevin reinterpreted some spicy remarks; Jim flew into a rage. I wondered, as I listened, whether Jim Shorts was a real person or not, finally deciding that he was not. He was, in fact, Kevin Matthews changing his voice. Wow! Oz's wizard. This is one clever radio show host, I concluded, who has crafted a short-tempered, irascible, indelibly negative curmudgeon as a contrast to his own slightly provocative foil.

Jim Shorts stands in a line of comic fictitious creations who strive to provoke smiles and laughter through outlandish actions, mendacity, and verbal abuse. They depend on the audience's recognition of the human state made ridiculous by its limitations. They mock; they deflate pretense; and sometimes they exploit low comedy or articulate the forbidden.

They have been crafted by some of our finest authors. We think of Boccaccio's Frate Cipolla, a Franciscan who cheats his trusting parishioners; Chaucer's pardoner, who openly admits fooling the public; Rabelais's Panurge, whose antics in Paris border indecency; and Shakespeare's Falstaff, who admits that "villainous company has been the spoil of me."[1] In contemporary, popular culture, we see the type in Jim Henson's muppet, Oscar the Grouch.

Almost every day for twenty years, Jim Shorts was heard on the radio by millions of people who knew him and loved him for his failings—and perhaps also for raising them above his querulous, pessimistic mien. And he was not alone; he had friends, as the show afforded a platform for other characters who appeared with him, mixing up the political, cultural, and religious discussion. In fact, they were a community who moved in and out of the radio world providing comic relief.

When I first met with Kevin Matthews and Father Mark Przybysz to discuss helping with a book about a statue of the Blessed Virgin Mary Kevin had found, I was happy to agree, but I had no idea that I was going to have to deal with Jim Shorts.

"So, will you write the book?" Kevin asked after he had explained the story of Broken Mary. Now, I am a writing professor whose job is to see that my students learn to write well in college. I do not do it for them.

---

1 William Shakespeare, *Henry IV, Part 1.* III. iii. 9.

"No," I said. "You will write the book. I will edit." I think that was a surprise, but it worked. Kevin immediately began to write enough background information about himself and his radio career to set up the reader for the extraordinary story of Broken Mary. That is why this book is divided into two parts.

A macaronic work that is at first autobiographical in outlining the career of an influential Midwestern radio personality, the book is primarily an account of the events surrounding the discovery and travels of the statue of Broken Mary and its effect on Kevin and others, but it is also interspersed with the imaginative rantings of Chicago's most well-known radio character. I did not know what would happen to Jim Shorts during the writing of the book, as he was still on air in podcasts, and, when I listened in, I found him to be anti-authoritarian with a less-than-noble vocabulary and irrational anger. He rarely said anything positive about anyone. It is his "on air" voice, dear reader, who greets you at the beginning of this book, and you will hear him periodically as you move through the story.

Sister Lucia Treanor, FSE
Franciscan Life Process Center

PART I

Radio Man

On Air

Jim Shorts here.

Some of you know me from my days on air in Chicago. I want to say that before you even think about reading this book, you need to know something. Without me there wouldn't be a radio personality named Kevin Matthews, and he certainly would never have gotten popular. Trust me, I *am* the show! I was hired to say things that he couldn't say, because he is a baby with very little spine. Period.

I am the voice. People have always loved it. Its raspy and gravelly flavor comes from an accident when I was ten years old. I was helping my father with aluminum siding, when a rain gutter slipped from his grip. I looked up, and the next thing I remember is lying in the emergency room with an eight-foot spout through my neck. The doctors told me that I would never speak again.

I was devastated. But my scrappy nature was ready to do battle to get my voice back and be heard. The doctors thought about transplanting a larynx, and since my blood type matched that of a recently dead baboon, my family decided it was my only hope. After nineteen hours in surgery and thirty-four days in a coma, I opened my eyes. When I spoke my first word, it was "Poop." So, for the next two years, I had to relearn language, including Canadian and four unknown dialects.

In the spring of 1981, I met Kevin Matthews. He had

heard me hosting the morning program at WFRT while he was driving through Fort Wayne, Indiana, and knew charm when he heard it. He invited me to lunch; we talked, but I had to pick up the tab. He is so cheap. I knew I was Kevin's ticket to a bigger radio market, because Jimmy DeCastro, the general manager of The Loop radio in Chicago, had already tried to hire me—only *me*—but I must have been glitched up, because I convinced him to hire Kevin and then fire him later when he wasn't looking. That silly ass has no idea how I saved his pathetic radio career. He is nothing but dead weight.

ONE

The Early Years

Pay no attention to Jim Shorts; he is a figment of the imagination. This story is being told by Kevin Matthews.

My mother often said that I would talk to myself as a child. She could see my mouth move, but heard no words. Then my head would turn to the sky, and I would say my "friends" were not from earth. "I play with spacemans, Momma. Can't you see them?"

Those early imaginative encounters in Pontiac, Michigan, provided a refuge for a little one lost in the 1960s confusion of family—Dad, Mom, older brother, big sister, and twin sister—and of the cars, the stores, the doctors, the yelling, the screaming, the hospitals, the cigarette smoke, the smell of alcohol, and the neighborhood, with its yelling, barking, riots, minority folk, and hatred. I experienced fear and loneliness with no one to play with except my friend, the Alien. And I was the only one who knew him by name. That was my secret.

You'd better wake up now, Kevin, said the Alien. *Your mother is calling, and if your dad comes up here, he will beat the shit out of one of us. Get up now.* I first met the Alien when I was four, maybe five years old. He would come to bed and protect me while I slept, and later when I was seven, he would walk me to school.

I used to hear old people say that they had to walk five miles every day to school and liked it. I hated walking to school. My twin sister and I went together every morning, sunshine, rain, or blizzard. It was a death march, filled with mental horrors. It always began the same way.

"We are leaving!" my sister and I would yell to our mother, and silently I asked, *Are you with me, Alien?*

Yes. I am, Kevin. Keep walking. You're fine. Trust me. Up the street we would go. The first house belonged to the Spencers. They were old and the husband was in a wheelchair with tubing hanging from his nose.

Is he going to die soon, Alien?

Pretty soon, Kevin. Keep walking, because you can't be late. The next houses belonged to some really weird monsters. After the Spencers' house was one with two drunks, a screaming woman with mascara stains and messy black hair and her sodden husband; they fought nightly in the front yard and haunted their passed-out house in the day.

Are they going to get drunk tonight, Alien?

Most likely, Kevin. Keep walking and watch your sister. As we continued, the houses we routinely passed got more frightening. Beside the drunks lived a short fat lady in a place covered with vines and trees.

I hate walking past this house, Alien. It scares me big time.

Remember, Kevin, we are walking on the other side of the block, and it is divided by the road. You are safe. No way would we ever walk on her side, in front of her yard, because she is always in the

6

bushes, on guard, ready to drag us into her creepy hidden home of leaves and thorns.

Then we went uphill, and our first block was nearly finished. We had triumphed over the wheelchair man, the drunks, and the vine lady by walking on the opposite side of the street. At the highest peak, we knew there were eight more to go. On Francis Street, we learned to turn right. This street was a busy two-lane and cars stopped for no one, especially pets. A big double-decker house stood at the top there, and we were joined by its kids, two dirty sisters in old and worn dresses, and an older brother, Alvin.

Why does he have yellow syrup on his hands? I questioned my friend. *His hands are always sticky.*

He does not wash that often, Kevin. It's not his fault. He's one of us, trust me. Keep walking, Kevin. School starts in twenty-five minutes. Hurry up and pay attention.

We walked past Mario Guzzo's house every morning. It was my job to stop and ring the doorbell, and out Mario and his younger sister, Maria, would come. They carried sack lunches, wore nice clothes, and had washed and combed hair. Momma Guzzo would wave and make sure they joined our herd of children safely. She reminded us all to be careful crossing the biggest street of all.

I hated crossing what I called "All Burn Avenue." It was a busy four-lane road with a traffic light and a safety patrolman, who was in the fifth grade. He wore a white belt that covered one shoulder and wrapped tightly around his winter coat. I wanted his job someday, because safety patrol boys got out of school early. I would have done anything to get out of school early.

Help me cross the street, Alien. I hate this street. I hate having to time this red light. Am I going to be killed this morning?

No. Watch your sister and run when I tell you to go. I stood in the center of the pack of kids, our toes on the edge of the curb. The light would stay green for hours, it seemed, and then change to yellow, while the traffic—all four lanes coming from both directions—would slowly come to a red light and stop.

Run now, but don't trip and fall. I would run as fast as I could up from the street and land, both feet at once, on the sidewalk, then spin around and look for my sister.

Did she make it?

I have hated Auburn Avenue all my life, because just two years later, one of my best friends was hit right where I had been walking every day. A car struck him in the head and for weeks he lay in St. Joseph Hospital. When he returned home, he was never the same: Part of his head was missing, and he could barely walk. He never remembered my name again.

The Alien and I knew we were getting close after the big crossing. There were only two easy blocks, one with a wreck of a home, but we could begin to hear the sounds of kids—some friends, some enemies—teachers, parents, the hubbub of school, just one block away.

Be careful now, Kevin. Walk. Don't run. Lots of parents are dropping off kids lucky enough to arrive at school in a warm car with real guardians as parents. Not you, not you and your sister; but I will protect you all day, every day, for the rest of your life.

I got to school every day just like that.

I hated school. I would just look out the window and watch birds fly by, wishing I were one of them. I wore my brother's and sisters' old clothes. I never wore socks. I took a bath once a week, and sometimes ate a school lunch if Dad remembered to leave money on the table. My sister and I were in the second grade, but in two different classrooms.

Why does my teacher hate me, Alien?

She doesn't hate you, Kevin. She just doesn't know how to teach you. She doesn't know how to deal with someone like you who has eye problems. She doesn't understand why you can't seem to learn your ABCs. And you don't pay attention. It's okay. I love you.

When the school day ended, my sister and I took a different way home. So we could drop off other kids who did not walk with us in the morning, our little herd processed in a circle. We still had to cross Auburn Avenue, but the return trip only had two weird and scary houses. Three blocks into the walk was the witch's house. From her attic window, a thin old woman watched without expression every child returning home from school. No one ever walked on her lawn. If anyone did, she would pound on the glass, banging the window with her long and bony fingers.

Is she a witch, Alien?

No, but everyone thinks she is. Just keep walking and don't turn around and look up at her. With two more blocks to go, the trek seemed forever. I knew I was almost home when I saw the Gibsons' house. It was white with a rusted red fence that kept in the biggest dog I had ever seen. Ace was a Great Dane. He would run along the fence and had the deepest bark. The owners were mean to him. I noticed that he never lived inside the house; his pen was behind the garage, a fenced-in dog run with an empty food dish and water bowl, a cold plywood doghouse, and dog turds covering the ground. I came to like Ace, until Animal Control took him away by force.

After the Gibsons, we were home, but it was not a safe house. If Dad brought home beer, I knew that he would begin yelling. The more beer he drank, the meaner he got. The only safety I had was my bed upstairs, away from the yelling. I remember to this day lying in bed, crying and pleading with the Alien, whose real name is God, *Please just let me die. Let me be with you. Please, please take me away.* The Alien has always been with me, from crossing the busy street to hearing my request for heaven.

TWO

Pontiac to Grand Rapids

Life in Pontiac was dark and violent, both outside and inside our 60 North Francis Street home. The neighborhood was failing then, and now has deteriorated so much that my brother found our home listed for sale recently for twenty-five hundred dollars—my bedroom, my hiding place, my first private church, sold for peanuts. I was born a Catholic and learned of Jesus there, and it was there at four years old that I prayed for help, to be taken to heaven; and there at six years old that I knew him as the voice of the Alien.

When I was in the fifth grade, we moved to "the country," Rochester, Michigan. At first I kept to myself, ready to pounce like a junkyard dog on anyone who even looked at me or my sister. I trusted no one at school, but gradually learned that the place was safe. I met some kids my age who rode bikes, built forts, and played baseball. As we grew, we also killed frogs with our BB guns, threw rocks at trains, and listened to music that our parents hated. Most of all, we discovered girls. These were the graced wonder years.

Although I later learned that I am dyslexic, I received average and below-average grades, and in high school I excelled in physical fitness, stayed straight—no drugs or alcohol—and worked at Perry Pharmacy in Troy. When I was fifteen, my brother, the floor manager, got me the gig so that I could buy a car and eat better food, since there was little to no extra support from our father. I was a great kid, really. Work taught me diligence, honesty, and humility. I was in a public arena and observing every kind of human being, but I hated school, except athletics and fitness—especially Marine Corps Fitness Training, which I perfected to prove to my father that he could no longer kick my ass, and to protect my mother and siblings from his physical and mental abuse. I did it so well that in my senior year, I was state champion and third in the nation competing in the Marine Corps Fitness Nationals. Decades later, on his deathbed, I forgave Dad for his harshness and his lack of respect for women. I whispered that it was okay to go. Within a minute, he was gone.

Perry Pharmacy on Big Beaver Road—as a young man, I included Big Beaver in any conversation I had with anyone who would listen, including family and teachers. I was a happy idiot, and the world was now all mine. I was chasing a young and beautiful girl whom I had met at Perry Pharmacy, and although the Marine Corps could not wait to enlist me and place me in the drill instructor training program in San Diego, and although I was ready, and although my high school counselor had urged me to go into the auto industry, I chased that girl all the way to college in Allendale, Michigan, near Grand Rapids. I arrived at Grand Valley State College in a 1972 red Volkswagen without any desire for an education or a college degree, but it was there that I was introduced to WSRX, student-run radio.

THREE

State College

My career in radio began by accident. My freshman roommate, Doug, a long-haired premed student with a closet pot
garden that I daily feared would be discovered, had a weekly
show on the college station, which was located in the student
center, and one day I trailed him there. I only had to follow
the smell of weed and sure enough, in the bottom of the
center was a tiny radio station with ten big watts of freedom,
ten watts that covered the entire campus, the small town of
Allendale, population three thousand, and if the wind was
blowing in the right direction, Grand Rapids.

I had no idea what I wanted to study—perhaps what they
now call movement science, maybe education—but the radio
station sure looked more appealing than the gym. During my
visit, I was introduced to the station manager, a graduating
senior. He hired me to file albums and type public service an-
nouncements. It was a boring job and I hated it; I wanted to
be on the air. I soon learned that this was one of the most
progressive underground radio stations in the country. Its
purpose was simple: Be different or go home. It played songs
and artists I had never heard before, such as John Coltrane,
Bob Marley, and Frank Zappa—anything antiestablishment.

One Friday night I got a phone call from the program
director, who was in the hospital after overdosing on tainted

pot and acid. Here was my big chance. He needed someone to do his show.

"Can you help me, man?"

"Did you say do your show?" A jazz show, from midnight until five, it was to begin in just two hours.

"Yeah."

"Okay. Sure." This was insane. I had never done a radio show before, and had no idea how the equipment worked, how to cue up records, or even how to turn on the main microphone. I was told, "Here is how you turn your microphone on and off. The records are here; play whatever you want, and don't swear." Midnight finally came and I carefully opened the microphone and said, "Hello. I am Kevin. It's dark out. It's raining. Here's Jim Morrison and the Doors." The turntable began to spin as "Riders on the Storm" went over the air and a radio personality was born.

I wish that I had a recording of my first radio show. It was frightening, yet beautiful. I had total freedom, alone in a dark room, speaking to . . . how many? Who was listening to my voice in the air, swirling through cornfields, into someone's car, as background noise in the dorms, in the darkness of the city? I could be anyone I wanted to be. Who would really know? It was, after all, theater of the mind.

I played as many jazz songs as I knew, about thirty minutes' worth, before pulling albums from the shelf that looked good, songs by performers I had heard my brother play in his Ford Torino—the Doors, Pink Floyd—and songs that sounded great late at night. After the first hour, my nervousness began to dissipate, and it disappeared altogether when I just became someone else. Who would know? The audience could not see me; they could only hear me. I began to talk slower and lower, and I introduced a new character during every break. By the end of the program, I had put these characters back in my head. We all left the studio, and I walked to my dorm room a young man with "friends" who knew what he was born to do: entertain people, and more importantly, entertain himself.

My stoned program director lived. If he had died, I would have gotten his show. Instead he was kicked out of school for poor grades and processing illegal drugs. The senior next in line got the gig, and I was on standby to take any air shift given to me. I spent four years at WSRX.

Grand Valley State was young, and professors were probably not vetted as they are today. The one overseeing the radio station was an old hippie who built synthesizers and played them on the air while tripping on LSD. His shows would go on for days. He brought caged birds into the studio and burned incense to mask his body odor. For the record, I never took drugs, because I simply did not need them. My imagination was busier than any acid trip.

As a freshman, my mind was a sponge. I took in everything: music, culture, hippies, preppie frat boys, jocks, students who got all As, students who failed, flower power, concerts on campus, protesters, keggers, toga parties, and most of all, authority challenges. By the time I was a senior, eight others and

I—some of whom went on to big radio careers—were running the radio station, and every student on campus and off listened to WSRX. It was the rebel on campus, and as a result, the college slowly began to defund it and change its direction to mimic National Public Radio, a station President Lubbers could enjoy. The writing was on the wall: Our senior class would be the last reign of terror. No more *Animal House* radio, because Dean Wormer was going to take it away.

I decided to take advantage of the situation. I hosted the morning show and had a huge college following. I told the students that President Lubbers had been murdered during the night and his body had been chopped up and tossed about the campus. To say the least, the campus police were summoned, I was taken off the air and given probation, and within a week the station plug was pulled, the studios vacated, and a student hair salon had replaced WSRX.

But by the following week, I had been hired at the Fox 101 in Grand Rapids, my first commercial radio gig. I got the job because of the entertainment I had provided to so many college students. I had dared to be different. It is true that you are as good as your last radio show, and my last one on WSRX was *Animal House* great.

FOUR

Comedy with a Clear Mind

I have never used cocaine or experimented with acid, mushrooms, or any hallucinogen. I never drank while performing stand-up comedy or playing with my band. After-parties were a different story; beer and cigarettes were my vice to decompress after performing.

One of my favorite comics was the late Sid Caesar. I was too young to watch his weekly television show, but later in life I discovered his comedic genius: his timing and flawless physical expressions. After reading his autobiography, *Where Have I Been?*, I could relate to his off-stage monsters, especially alcohol. In addition, Sid was a perfectionist onstage; he rehearsed again and again, something I demanded from my band and from my stand-up performances.

I remember the first time I ever saw a live comedy show. A small club called the Comedy Den opened above a skating rink in Grand Rapids. A friend of mine had invited me to attend the grand opening to watch open mike night. The year was 1979.

We arrived at the weird, giant ice rink, which was freezing cold. Whistles were blowing, with pucks hitting the wooden boards, and kids in hockey uniforms were practicing to be the next Gordie Howe. We had to walk around the rink to enter through big black velvet drapes. A red exit sign led us to a large staircase made of wood, which made climbing noisy. It was still cold. At the top of the stairs, we entered a set of double doors, and a thin, toothless door manager checked our IDs (drinking age in Michigan at that time was eighteen) and stamped our hands. There was no cover, and glasses of beer cost a quarter.

We found a table for two just a few rows back from the stage, which was surrounded by red velvet drapes. A yellow neon sign reading THE COMEDY DEN hung from the wall directly behind the microphone, which stood center stage. The room held about eighty people; a hundred could be wedged in if the owner ignored state fire codes, which he did constantly. Each table had a red lit candle, and table tents promoted comics coming in later weeks. Cigarette smoke began to fill the air while the patrons talked softly, waiting for the show to begin, everyone anticipating what was to come. *What is this thing called stand-up comedy in our town?* The room was full and the clock said 8:00 p.m.; it was showtime. The jazz that was playing through the house speakers abruptly stopped. The toothless man spoke on a microphone near the door next to shelves holding empty plastic beer pitchers.

"Ladies and germs, welcome to the Comedy Den of Grand Rapids. During tonight's performance, please keep your table conversations down to a minimum. Hecklers will be asked to leave. And now, here's your host and emcee for this evening, Joe Dunkel."

The emcee took to the stage, touched the mike stand, pulled out the microphone, and began to entertain the crowd. Within seconds, he had the audience laughing as he did an impression of an old man putting on a hat and mumbling. He was getting laughs.

Suddenly, I was in my parents' kitchen in Pontiac, entertaining drunk neighbors, walking barefoot, walking on my toes, impersonating President Kennedy, thinking if I made people laugh, it meant they liked me. Watching Joe Dunkel act like an old man wearing a hat turned on a comedy switch, which was acceptance. *If I make Dad laugh, he can't hit me.*

At the time of this event, I was doing late-night radio, but had never seen anything like this. As I sat in my seat watching this guy, I thought, *I can do this.* I was mesmerized. Throughout the night, I saw comic after comic enter the stage for open mike night to give a three-to-five-minute performance. Comics used their time to tune up and try new material, without pay. Then the emcee would flash a light from the back of the room, which meant "Get off. Your time is up." I later found out that you obeyed that rule or you never worked this or any club again.

Finally the endless line of comics stopped and the emcee introduced the evening's headliner. It was Thursday night, and the headliner was to be there for the rest of the week. I can't remember his name, but he "killed," as we say in the business. As soon as he stepped onstage, he owned it, and the material coming from his mouth was funny. He unleashed verbal napalm for forty-five minutes, blowing away the emcee and most of the comics before him. *That's what I want to do. I can say things onstage that I can't say on the radio! This is perfect.* I could imagine the comedy club as a gym. *How do I sign up for open mike night?*

The show ended, and I immediately introduced myself to the emcee and owner of the club, who knew my name because of my nighttime radio program. I was just beginning in radio and did not have the following I would have years later, but Joe invited me to return next Thursday and signed me up for open mike night: two minutes; no pay; me and at least five others on the list who wanted to be comics.

I was number three to go up. I was not afraid of standing in front of people, but like a junkyard dog, I knew if they hurt me, I would just kick everyone's ass in the club and set it on fire. My name was introduced.

"Ladies and germs, this next comic is making his stage debut. You may have heard him on the radio. Please welcome Grand Rapids' very own, Kevin Matthews." I had come up with three simple ideas as I walked through the crowd, hearing the light applause. *Wow! I am getting applause.*

As soon as I stepped onstage, I felt safe, even though the bright lights blinded me, allowing me to see the first four rows of the audience only. If I held my hands up over my eyes, I could see the entire smoke-filled room: the audience, the sheep in the back, the last-minute arrivals. Those sitting and power-drinking way in the back were the hecklers, pussies who would not dare to sit up front. I took to the stage with fake confidence, wearing a gold jacket, a black T-shirt that displayed the Buzzcocks' logo, tight black pants, and used white prom shoes. The punk movement scared the majority of people. Most of this audience was listening to disco, or Boston records. But I loved punk music and anything rude by Frank Zappa.

So as I stood onstage for the very first time, looking like Sid Vicious of the Sex Pistols, I took the microphone from the stand and placed the stand behind me. I moved to the very front of the stage and looked down at the tables, giving the people nothing but silence. Slowly I looked behind me, to my right, and to my left, and then turned my attention to the dropped ceiling above me. I was eating my two minutes up quickly with silence, and the audience, considering the way I was dressed and observing the stage surroundings, started to giggle uncomfortably.

"What a shit hole this place is! I feel like I am in my dad's basement." The room roared with laughter. I then reflected on our basement in Pontiac, and Dad's attempt to remodel it. I ended my three-minute set doing an impression of Dad yelling for toilet paper, as I slowly walked toward the bathroom, opened the door, reacted to the odor, and tossed in a new roll as if it were a grenade killing Germans in WWII. Suddenly, my eyes were blinded by a bright flashlight from the back of the room: My time was up and I had to leave the stage immediately.

"I hate you all. I am Kevin Matthews," I said and walked

off the stage. The applause was stimulating; it was like feeding a lion bloody red meat, and I wanted more. The emcee and owner of the club came to me after the show and asked whether I would return. He offered me no pay, but three free drinks, and I said yes.

I loved performing stand-up comedy. I was finally free onstage to talk about anything that came to my mind, content I could never get away with on the radio. This tiny comedy stage was my boxing ring. I was soon the opening act for comedy headliners who were beginning to gain popularity in America. The only other comedy club in Michigan at the time was the Comedy Castle in Detroit. The only other comedy club in the Midwest was Zanies in downtown Chicago. I will save my comedy stories for another time. Suffice it to say, I performed in Kalamazoo, Detroit, and Chicago.

My greatest comedy teacher of all time was the late Bill Hicks, who was once a roommate of the late Sam Kinison, a giant in the world of comedy. Bill and I became great friends and would perform together as often as possible in Chicago. I had him on my radio program countless times. He performed at one of my largest outdoor parties while in Chicago, and along with Joe Walsh, Styx, and my entire morning crew, he entertained more than thirty thousand screaming Kevheads at Alpine Valley in Wisconsin.

The bottom line is courage. Stand-up comedy was just another way of releasing anger and daring a live audience to think differently, for just sixty minutes.

On Air

Jim Shorts here again.

If you are still reading this book, you are a doofus. I told you that Kevin Matthews was nobody without me, and he has not even mentioned my name. I *am* the show. People love me. I don't know why Jimmy DeCastro did not fire him as we agreed. If he can't tell the story right, I will. Do you know how my friends and I came to be?

Kevin was never afraid of making a fool of himself, or me, or my friends, because he thinks that radio is theater of the mind. When he was young, he liked to make his family laugh, especially his dad. (He thought it was better than getting beaten with the belt.) Mostly, though, he has always hated authority, those he calls "the mean people"—people who make others, especially women and children, cry.

When he was a senior at Grand Valley State College, the Federal Communications Commission and the college administration shut WSRX down, because they did not like our antiauthoritarian ways. The campus officials told us—Kevin and my friends—to leave. We were an embarrassment and a threat to society. I am proud of this accusation. I know it's because I am so real that I *am* a threat to society. Like many of Kevin's friends, I *like* to challenge authority. They are the "thought police."

Kevin's first professional radio gig was at the Fox 101, a hip album-rock station that covered all of West Michigan.

It was part time, but my friends Officer Steelballs and Little Darrnell and I kept him on air. His sense of humor and impeccable timing and imagination had nothing to do with it.

I am his most popular character. He may say that I am a total pig who tells it like it is, but in reality the truth flows from this five-foot-seven hulk from Fort Wayne, Indiana. Kevin tells people that I am fat, wear glasses, pass gas, and was hit by a car twice as a child, which is true except for the glasses. When I am on air, I taunt management, call them stupid, and am a hero to my audience.

My friend Devon, who came to life in Chicago, was born when Kevin was watching the race riots just outside Detroit at the age of six. He is a black space alien who basically hates all white people, yet loves Jesus. Kevin could never preach on any commercial radio station, but Devon does. Devon has sympathy for Kevin and knows how the world is going to end.

And then there's Darrnell. Like Devon and me, Darrnell is a voice of truth, but he lives in a politically correct world.

I think Kevin hates radio general managers, program directors, and any kind of radio authority. The *only* good thing about him is that he cares about his audience. He loves anyone who's struggling, the young fellow working two jobs—because he is one of them, having managed jobs night and day.

Cut it, Jim. That's enough of that. Stop yammering and go chase yourself.

FIVE

Grand Rapids to Chicago

After working in commercial radio at WLAV Grand Rapids and then for a year in St. Louis, I was hired by the WLUP-FM (97.9), which immediately bought WLUP-AM (1000) Chicago, known as The Loop, where I remained as a radio personality from 1987 to 1998, creating content that included character voices such as those of Jim Shorts, Devon, Darrnell, and Cliff Dic—people of all types: businessmen and washerwomen, sacred clerics and profane quacks, libertarians and rednecks. I impersonated presidents from Ronnie to Clinton, and celebrities galore. The common man spewed from my mouth. I became involved in my community and was accessible to my audience—never above them, always with them. I was a listener doing radio, a wind talker, who before each radio show asked for God's help.

These were challenging and wild years, a tornado of living—of loud, uncensored comedy, of concert stages and travel, of hunting and fishing, of Ted Nugent and the Chicago Bears (every Bear), of "making every round count" and number one ratings, of Indian Guides and Ninja Turtles, of the Bulls winning and the NHL, of partying and family, of prime rib and limos, and of making the *Chicago Tribune's* readers' "Best of" poll again. It was one giant, big-big ride.

Radio was never work for me; it was an escape, and I would let people listen, dream, and enter a world of imagination. It may sound cliché, but if you find something you love to do, it's not work. I hated waking up every morning at four thirty, but once I sat up and put my feet on the floor, it was wheels up. Showtime. I could not wait until I entered the air studio. I had a rule: No rehearsing. And another rule: Always tell the truth on the air. I would ask my staff, "What is the biggest secret you have? What don't you want anyone to know?" The truth is the best radio, the best form of entertainment.

During my early years in Chicago, my air staff and I were young. I had two small children at home, and my producer was black and single. I had a female sports announcer who was trying to get pregnant, and my news announcer feared that I would ruin his credibility, which I did every morning. I always included the audience. We were one big intoxicated family, laughing so hard that it made breathing difficult. I invited my audience to stop by the studios and talk. Once while I was on air, four Chicago Bears kicked in my studio door, duct-taped me to my chair, took Magic Markers and covered my face, and tore off my shirt. My audience heard every moment. Then they wheeled me downstairs and left me tied up on Michigan Avenue.

My radio program was simply an escape, a theater of the mind. Hear me daily, or come see my band. Watch me do stand-up comedy. I would vacation with my audience, and my audience would invite me and my radio crew over for pool parties. I was invited to weddings, birthday parties, and even funerals. I simply grew up with my audience and they grew up with me. Every week while broadcasting, I spoke to millions of people I called Kevheads in Chicago, the third-largest radio market in America. It was never work, but play, and always for the love of entertaining. In 2013, I was named one of the top twenty-five radio personalities in the past twenty-five years. I would never have won this award without my loyal audience that I love so much.

My signature bit was "free bird," and I am often asked how yelling it at the right moment during other people's concerts began. This vocal gesture has gotten worldwide attention. If a reporter were to ask Mick Jagger of the Rolling Stones today, "Have you ever heard anyone in the audience yell 'free bird'?" he would answer, "Of course." Even *The Wall Street Journal* did a front-page story on its history.

It started out in 1982 as an inside joke between a pot-smoking hippie radio friend and me. His program had had to endure constant play requests from kids, and one in particular kept asking for "Free Bird" by Lynyrd Skynyrd. Months later, I suggested that a caller to my show yell "free bird" during a poignant moment in Florence Henderson's performance at a dinner theater. He did and reported back to my audience, setting off a veritable train of "free bird" interruptions that lasted for years. I added a "free bird" to my stand-up comedy routine, and my band, Ed Zepplin, played "Free Bird" at the end of my shows. Singer-songwriter Jimmy Buffett's "Bama Breeze" pays homage to "free bird" in its lyrics.

During this time, communications—music, print, television—was all changing. The Internet, a wooden horse, had entered Troy. I had thought that I was working in an industry that was guaranteed never to die, but I was not blind. I saw Odysseus' troops sneaking out of the horse, and I began moving toward safety. Few followed me. I have always embraced new technology, and I was one of the first radio personalities to have a website. Kevhead.com grew rapidly, with two hundred thousand weekly visits. There were people from Europe, Asia, and Alaska, so I knew the world was watching me in real time, but everyone else was asleep like the Trojans: ABC, radio general managers, radio consultants, record reps, newspapers, TV. And so the radio industry was attacked by the Internet, and so was I. Even though I'd had the number one morning show for men age twenty-five to fifty-four for five straight ratings periods (i.e., one and a half years) and the highest ratings ever, I was fired in a panic to deal with Internet competition. WLUP, which had become WMVP, was sold to ABC Radio and became part of ESPN sports.

The next three years were spent at WXCD-FM (94.7). That later became WZZN-FM and now is WLS-FM. At one time I was speaking to ten million listeners weekly, making more money than I ever thought possible, and entertaining sold-out crowds at every venue in the Midwest doing stand-up and playing with my band. I performed in front of sixty-five thousand fans in Grant Park. I traveled around the world, met the rich and famous, had a Navy SEAL's baby named after me, and helped countless charities. I entertained hundreds of thousands of people with shows inside prisons, army bases, and backyards.

I was hired by CBS Chicago's WCKG-FM (105.9) in 2002 with Kevhead.com, which continued its global growth. My audience followed me and so did a million dollars in advertising. My promotions became legendary: comedy jams, my band, my BBQ throw-downs, my golf outings. Oh, my golf outings. I was kicked out of ten country clubs in ten years. We destroyed these places, literally. Strippers, booze, broken windows, damaged greens, food fights, nudity, and more nudity. All for children's charities. I was as popular as Aerosmith and on the same destructive path. When CBS wanted to cut my pay in half and take the rights and Web traffic for Kevhead.com, I said no.

I was out of radio for more than a year. Ultimately the station went downhill. Concern for content and listeners was replaced by consultant knee-jerk reactions and focus group ideas. Howard Stern's move to Sirius satellite radio was ignored. "That will never work," they said. "So what if they don't play commercials? They play too much music." Once the most respected giant in the industry, the station is now nothing more than a garage sale, a silent, dead giant. From the vantage point of fourteen years, I can see that traditional radio will never recover. When I visit Chicago these days, I scan the dial and listen to old friends like Steve Dahl. It brings a smile to my heart to hear Bob Stroud or Terri and the crew at WXRT. I think of my former producers Doc (Simpson), Shemp (Mark DeYoung), Chunga (Mitch Rosen), Geli Corbett and Duji (Susan Catanese), and managers who took a chance and hired me decades ago, Larry Wert, Jimmy DeCastro, Greg Solk, and Jeff Schwartz. I miss Wolfman Jack and John Alan, and I think of Ed Buchanan every time I see someone drink a Miller Lite. With these people and my audience, we *did* change the face of radio.

Technology has changed the way we now are entertained. I no longer need a radio station; I have my own studio to reach listeners globally. I still love making folks laugh, but now I attribute my success to God, without whom none of this would have happened. But before I leave Chicago, I need to speak of one of its great benefits: getting to spend time with Huck-So-Ta, a "grandfather" to whom I became connected in a "making of relative" ceremony.

Indians

The first time I ever saw an Indian—that's what Dad called them—was from the backseat of his new Buick. I was thirteen and on vacation with my parents and twin sister. I hated this vacation, wanting to be home with my big brother, who was having parties with beer, cool tunes, and hot older girls with tans, who thought that I was cute, squeezed my cheeks, smiled, and said, "You're so sweet. Let's make out."

Instead I was in the backseat with my sister, while my mom and dad were up front smoking, listening to the worst music recorded at the time, looking at a big map of Montana, and yelling as they drove down the longest dirt road in America.

Suddenly, my dad began slowing down his prized Buick from seventy miles per hour to a crawl. "Look, kids. Indians—real Indians!" The Indian—there was only one—was just a young Native American girl, about seven, playing with an empty box. She had dust in her hair and covering her white tank top. She wore red shorts, had no shoes, and her bare red feet were covered in white Montana dust. My parents waved.

The little girl was on my side of the car, and as we inched up, her eyes looked at me, black as coal—no smile, no wave, motionless. I turned my head, looking at her from the big rear window. She just stared, and my dad sped up, covering the child in a cloud of dust, gravel spraying her like buckshot from a shotgun. I continued to look through the rear window until she was out of sight.

"Kids, we are going to see lots of Indians on this trip, maybe some buffalo, too!" exclaimed my dad. "Keep a lookout, kids. They might start shooting arrows at us." *God, I want to be home.*

I will never forget that child covered in dust, or her stare, her black eyes, her long, black, dusty hair, playing with the only toy she had—a big, broken brown box. Without saying a word, our eyes had connected. I knew her; she was me.

SEVEN

Grandpa Sana

I was destined to meet more Native Americans in the years to come, people from not only Montana but also Wyoming, South Dakota, Arizona, Utah, Minnesota, Kentucky, and Tennessee, those whose ancestors had walked on the Trail of Tears. One of them, an Iroquois from Niagara Falls, New York, would become my greatest teacher and my best friend. He never asked me for a dime. Everything he did during this time was simply for the Creator God. His name was Turhan Clause.

When he was a baby, Turhan's feet crisscrossed, so his parents gave him the spiritual name Turhan, or "Crossing Feet." Like many Native Americans, he made a living building the highest skyscrapers in New York City, including the Twin Towers. A steelworker, he walked the sky and then traveled the world, teaching and learning about different people, cultures, and religions. My time with this peaceful man was no accident, as I had always wanted to be the Indian when I played Cowboys and Indians as a kid, and my favorite animal that walks the earth is the buffalo.

Grandpa Sana, as I called him, would always carry his pipe, which many people call a peace pipe. He was and always will be a pipe carrier. My Lakota brothers and sisters call the pipe, as did Grandpa, "chanupa wakan" (cha-new-pa wa-con), "the holy chanupa," and "the great mystery."

"The chanupa is all that is male and all that is female," he told me one day. "It has two parts, the long wooden stem and the stone bowl."

"What does it mean?" I asked him.

"The bowl represents all that is male. When the stem is inserted into it, what is female. It becomes one, male and female, all that is. We now can pray together, as one, with the Creator God." Grandpa had great respect for women: They were smarter, and the eldest woman always had the final say when they gathered, in everything.

"Men are pigs," he once told me during a pipe ceremony. "Women create life; they give birth to the world. Men are pigs; they destroy this very same life, and they carry the dead to graves." Grandpa taught me to walk gently when you walk the earth, "for she too is female, and very old and delicate."

"Walk gently and with bare feet when you walk on her," he would repeat again and again. "You see, everything is male and female. Even what is above you in the sky. The sun is male; the moon is female." So when Grandpa said men are pigs, it hit home. He was admitting that we males destroy life, while the females give life. The truth is painful to hear, but observe the world today. Who continues to give birth? Women. Who on this planet kills and destroys what God has given us? Men.

While working in Chicago, I attended a Catholic church, and my wife and I raised our children Catholic. I liked my church. I gave thanks to God, but I loved the outdoors. I hunted and fished as often as possible. I was a great bow-hunter. Grandpa loved it when I told him once, "Grandpa, I shot a bear with my bow!"

"A-ho," he said, nodding his head. It meant that he was thankful. "That bear was born for you. You now have that bear's spirit with you. It is good, another gift from God."

"Grandpa, why are you so happy all the time?" I asked.

"Because God has given me everything I need. When you wake up, Kevin, try and out-give God." Think of that. What a goal to have, to try and out-give God every day!

Spending time with Grandpa was amazing. I often had him in the broadcast studio with me, and he would sit and laugh. "Laughter is good medicine. You're a medicine man, a wind talker, Kevin." He said that because I talked into a microphone that went into the wind like the Navajo code talker of WWII. My radio station personnel looked at Grandpa and me cautiously, wondering, *What is Kevin doing with these Native Americans? Is he smoking pot in those pipes? Why does he talk about hunting on the air so much? Why is Kevin doing a fundraising event for the Pine Ridge reservation?* Once again, I was pushing the radio envelope, but all I was really doing was living life without blinders—learning, thinking, and most of all, giving thanks to God.

Once while we were walking in a beautiful field, waist-deep in prairie grass, Grandpa stopped and said, "Kevin, the earth that you walk on, she is your floor. The sky above you is your ceiling, and the four winds—the north, the south, the east, and the west—this is your church, and it's very big." My time with Grandpa was significant.

EIGHT

Reclaiming the Land

I introduced Grandpa to a friend I had met, basically a total stranger, who had invited me to bowhunt deer on his forty-acre property seventy miles west of downtown Chicago, just outside Sandwich, Illinois. His name was Andy, and I had known his brother when I was living in Hinsdale.

Andy was a mechanic who worked on big equipment for the local gas company. He had purchased the property when it was nothing more than a landfill, a dumping ground for abandoned cars and washing machines. A dreamer, Andy saw the beauty in this land when he married his wife. He mentally eliminated the rusted washing machines, old cars, and trash, airbrushing them out of the picture, and then he began actually doing it. After work each day, he removed the garbage by hand; night by night, weekend by weekend, his property came to life, returning to its natural glory, a rolling beauty with mammoth mounds of dirt covered in wild grass and native flowers.

So I introduced Andy to Sana Turhan Clause, who then introduced him to an old friend, a Lakota named Chief Joseph Chasing Horse, who was a direct descendant of the great Lakota elder Crazy Horse. From him, Andy learned that the mounds were ancient burial grounds.

I invited Sana and Joseph to speak at the Chicago Outdoor Sports Show in Rosemont, a huge event that attracts thousands each year. They spoke to those attending about respecting the hunting grounds, the earth, and the environment that many take for granted. The discussion was a popular attraction, and their three seminars were sold out and well accepted.

I remembered this on a beautiful Saturday afternoon, when the sky was so blue and the wind was still for the evening's ceremony, perfect for the fire I had already started hours ago. Puffs of white clouds peppered the sky, and the sun would be completely out of sight within hours. Sana and I would be there late into the night, praying. Indian prayer to Creator God is powerful.

NINE

Do You *Truly* Believe?

Many people knew how strongly Native Americans believed in the power of prayer, and so when a dear friend whose daughter had been ravaged by spinal cancer and was given only a year to live determined that her dying without a fight was not an option, I resolved to help.

"Kevin, can your Native American friends help my daughter?"

"I don't know whether they can, but I do know that the power of prayer and believing in God can," I said. "I will make some phone calls." I asked a dear Cherokee grandmother for advice, and she immediately contacted a Lakota medicine man from North Dakota.

It was decided that the medicine man and Cherokee grandmother would hold a ceremony for the little girl in three weeks. I called the father in California and told him that Sana had arranged for a healing ceremony in the lodge outside Chicago that I had built for him and the elders years ago. When the day arrived, the father, a friend of his, and the little girl, who was too sick to walk, met the Cherokee grandmother, whom I had not seen in years, the medicine man, and his two friends. They had traveled in a car rusted with age. There we were, a group of strangers, all for a little girl who was dying of cancer.

The medicine man, an elder with long gray hair, began: "Good things are here. The Creator God is with us." He gathered all of us in, making a motion with his hands to sit on the ground and listen carefully. The father sat first, and his daughter was carefully handed to him. He held her lovingly in his lap and arms. She said nothing, and showed no fear, but her sickness, her tired and worn body, was apparent to us all. We sat in a circle.

"Whoever does not believe that this little girl will be healed by the Creator God must leave now," the medicine man said calmly, but with authority. Silently we looked at one another, but no one stood up to leave.

"Again, I tell you, all of you here, if you do not believe, if you have any doubt that this little girl will be healed by the Creator God, you must leave now." We looked at one another again, and again no one moved. I trusted these people gathered for this child.

Looking at me, he began by raising his eyebrows, and then nodding his head. "A-ho," he said. I had heard that before, and knew what it meant: He was talking to Spirit.

"Yes, good," replied the elders.

Who is he talking to? Does he want me to leave? Did I do something wrong?

"You need to let your grandfather go. He's okay, but you keep him coming back again and again. Don't be sad; let him go," he advised, looking directly at me in front of the entire circle. My eyes began to tear up.

How does this man I never met before know about Grandfather?
"Let him go," said the elder. "He is with us today because you asked, but after today, let him go to Creator God's land. Stop being sad." I sat in shock and simply said yes to this medicine man from North Dakota. (My beloved grandfather had "crossed over" many months before, and I did miss him dearly.)

"So if you truly believe, then let's all pray for this little girl, in this holy circle, in the lodge today."

I had prayed here many times before. We entered the lodge and again sat quietly in a circle. The father was the last. He was given his daughter, exhausted by her battle with cancer, by one of the fire keepers from North Dakota. The ceremony began and lasted less than an hour. We prayed together silently, while the elder spoke softly in Lakota. I recognized many of the words: "Creator God," "yes," "thank you," and "I understand."

"She is good. She is healed and will live for many years and become an old woman, a good woman, who will help many. Go all of you and walk the earth." The medicine man left the lodge and the elder to his left crawled out, each person following the last until the lodge was empty.

It is tradition to eat after a ceremony and talk friendly to one another, a time to learn more about the people gathered. No one questioned what had happened that day, because everyone believed that Creator God had healed the child. It was a lesson in faith, believing in the power of God without question.

The father, his daughter, and his friend left after eating a simple meal, thanking all who came, especially the medicine man and the elders from North Dakota. An elder never asks for money for any kind of ceremony, because prayer is free, and no one should ever charge to pray. I had learned that long ago from Sana. I was the last to leave and assured the medicine man that I understood what he had said about letting Sana leave. (I did offer to pay for a new set of tires and gas for the travels. It was my gift to him, because I wanted him to return to North Dakota safely.) He nodded like a buffalo and said, "A-ho." Thank you.

I will never forget that day, the father, or the girl, who is still in California. She has physical challenges, but I hope she lives for many years. When we pray, I learned from the Lakota, we need to believe totally that our prayers will be answered. More important, we must believe in God without question.

Sana had known his time on earth was coming to an end, because his diabetes was killing him. So months before he crossed over, he told me, "When I enter Creator God's land, if you need to talk to me, during a full moon say my name and I will go sit on the moon and we can talk." To this day, when I see a full moon, I smile and say, "Hello, Sana." I have talked to him for hours, staring at the moon. Do I believe Sana sits on the moon? Yes. In heaven, anything is possible.

I spent years with Sana and I will never forget what he gave me: the ability to talk freely, to pray, and always to believe, to know that you are loved, from birth, by God. My favorite teachings are the following:

"We are all related."

"Stop saying you are white, I am red, he is black, he is yellow. Our hearts are all one color: red."

"When you are born, you cry the breath of life; as you get old, each breath becomes a prayer; and soon you will breathe no more on earth."

"There is no such thing as time. It was created by man. We move in a circle with the sky world, with all that is."

"We own nothing; all that we have is our flesh and our blood."

"Do the best you can and you will have done enough in the eyes of Creator God."

TEN

Chicago to Grand Rapids

In 2005, it was time for me to leave Chicago and return to my roots, back to the starting line to begin again. I was becoming predictable in Chicago, and the radio environment was changing as it reacted to the Internet and alternative platforms of entertainment, especially satellite radio. I decided to return to West Michigan to master technologies that would make my craft better. I knew that content was key.

I became the morning host at 97 LAV-FM in Grand Rapids. Ratings and advertising increased instantly. I could be heard on the World Wide Web. I learned the art of production, multitrack editing, and programming software. I was given the title of Director of Program Development. I helped put new radio stations on the air, as well as new formats and specialized radio features and promotions. I was working nonstop, and eighty-hour workweeks became common. Of the stations I was putting on the air, one in particular captured my heart, and I loved it. All this made me a better broadcaster, but the move came with painful consequences.

My daughter was in her final years of high school in Chicago, and it was important that she receive her diploma with her peers. Also, the housing market was crashing throughout America, and our home stayed on the market for nearly two years while I commuted to Michigan. During this time, I prayed for guidance for me and my family. I thought about serving the Lord. I had the power of the microphone and I wanted to use it in a positive way, to help the community and to have fun, but also to quietly tell my audience to follow God. Throughout my radio career, I was practically forbidden to talk about Christianity or my sincere love for God, so I created promotions that benefited charities. For decades, I supported children, police and fire, our military, and churches—all denominations, including extensive work with Native Americans—as often as possible, but was I really being honest with God? I have always been honest on air, because I love my audience and they trust me, but my courage to say Jesus' name over the air was weak—almost silent—and hidden from the public. In spite of this, God has never abandoned me. Throughout my return, something kept urging me deep in my soul, saying, "Will you deny me publicly?"

While I was reclaiming my popularity in Grand Rapids for five years, I was also returning to friends. Many of them had become successful business leaders. One was a priest.

"Will you deny me publicly?" I continued to hear.

"Kev used to be funny, but now he's all into Jesus. Time to change stations," I could imagine my listeners saying. It had been decades since my last confession, but here I was reunited with, of all people, a priest, Father Mark Przybysz. It was time to rinse out my soul. I had been aware of God's presence since I was four years old. He had provided me with a family, a wonderful career, and everything I'd ever needed, yet I continued to ignore him. It was time to come clean, to admit that I was a con, just a weekend warrior who was afraid of being called a "Jesus freak."

Father Mark and I had collaborated when my career was exploding in Chicago. I had returned home to help raise money for his church, St. Anthony of Padua, on the Polish West Side of Grand Rapids. We both loved cooking, so we thought a food challenge between us would attract fans and parishioners. It did, and we raised a huge amount of money. After the event, Father Mark had returned to his parish and I to Chicago.

It was wonderful seeing him at my welcome home party in 2005. Here I was, surrounded by fans and the business leaders of West Michigan, all clapping and so excited to see me, including Father Mark. Waving his arms, yelling "free bird," he got my attention. I gave him a big hug and we both could not wait to cook again, to help another charity, including his church.

"Will you deny me publicly?" Here I was standing face-to-face with a priest, who would play such a role in my life, and who was the caretaker of a church that would play an even a bigger role in the years to come. Father Mark and I booked a lunch date to catch up. He was fascinated by the work I had done with Native Americans. He invited me to speak to a group of his parishioners about my journey, and I was able to display the many gifts given to me by tribal nations.

I was happy. Finally I had a church again, one that welcomed me with open arms, a church filled with beautiful people of all ages and all colors and surrounded with love. I attended Mass as often as possible, but on the weekends I traveled to Chicago to be with my family, and to look at a FOR SALE sign that would never say SOLD.

On air, I welcomed Father Mark as often as I could, promoting the culinary events we created.

"You're a great priest, but you sure can't barbecue."

"I heard what you said today, Kevin. Remember, God's listening."

I thought about the question: "Are you going to deny me publicly?" Here I was, on the air with a priest, talking about church, helping raise money for charity, but I was not thanking God or praising Jesus. Not even a simple thank-you publicly. How sad. I was afraid my general manager would yell at me: "Stop talking about this Jesus crap on the air."

Before I could have Father Mark on air again, or before we did any work together, I needed him to hear my confession, one-on-one. The last time I was in a confessional, it was a dark box divided by a bamboo screen, the shadow of the priest, head nodding, hearing me—an eight-year-old—admitting to stealing pop and gum from the local grocery store. Now, decades later, I sat with a priest—a friend, but still a priest *in persona Christi*. God was listening, and so was my dead grandfather.

"Bless me, Father, for I have sinned. It's been 1964 since my last confession."

Father simply looked into my eyes and said, "What is your confession?"

What came out of my mouth was true sadness, embracement, and shame. I quietly said, "I cannot pray to the Virgin Mary. I am not worthy; she represents all who are female, including my wife, daughter, mother, and sisters—all who are female. I walk fast with my head down when I pass her statues. I am a pig; I am not worthy of her presence. I am so sorry and ask for forgiveness."

The whole world knows my failings. Though I always made it clear that I have never cheated on my wife, I surrounded myself with strippers, more strippers, wet T-shirt contests, pole dancing contests, and strip club openings. Offenses against women. I may be able to say I never cheated, but my eyes and hands surely have. That girl Jell-O wrestling during one of my comedy jams was someone's daughter. Those topless ball washers at the golf outings were, too. Those hookers on *The Jenny Jones Show*—they have fathers. I certainly have had a rousing career of parties, concerts, golf outings, and girls in the studio, on air, eating giant hot dogs with no buns. Great fun, but at whose expense? Lacking an understanding of the dignity of women, I had become my dad, and I was sorry.

But what a miracle! In his great mercy, through the sacrament of reconciliation and the authority of Father Mark, God forgave me. And I knew that Mary did, too.

ELEVEN

The Presence of Mary

Father Mark had simply said, "You are forgiven," and for the first time in my life, I was free of serious sin. Until that moment, I had never felt good enough for anyone—certainly not in the eyes of God, Jesus, and most of all, Mary—but now I did, as I humbly left the confessional.

When I walked through the church, I stopped to gaze into the eyes of a painted statue of Mary, poised to comfort the afflicted. Until then, I could never look at her, or at any representation of the Blessed Virgin. Her hands were reaching out, extending the calmness of her face. I finally allowed myself to see her beauty, a mother's love radiating from a graceful piece of art, this statue of the mother of Christ. Staring at it evolved into meditation on my confession, and I realized something important: It was my fault. I was the one who had kept myself from Mary, God, Jesus, and love. I had chained myself for all these years to the walls of hell, walls filthy with guilt and shame. Now, for the first time in my life, I felt peace, and I thought someone was gently whispering, "I have never left you. You let go of my hand, but I've got you again."

I returned to my truck and sat in silence, suddenly keenly aware of my situation: There I was in Grand Rapids, living alone in a small rental house on the north side of town. My wife was in Chicago with my daughter, and my son was in

Los Angeles. I was away from my wife, my son, my daughter, my dog, Charlie—my family. I was separated from everyone I loved, waiting for our house to sell, waiting for graduation, waiting for this, waiting for that, waiting, waiting, waiting. All for a job in radio. This pain had been brought on by me, not by God, not by Jesus, not by Mary, not by my wife, not by my son, not by my daughter, not by anyone but me. Enough!

I turned the ignition. As I put the truck into drive, I remember saying one more prayer before I left the church parking lot: "Jesus, help me now. What am I to do?"

I drove home in silence and, to my surprise, soon felt a profound sense of reconciliation and such a surge of love. I knew then that we would sell the house; my daughter would graduate and attend college. My son is such a talented musician; my wife is strong. We would be fine. I had been blessed in so many ways.

I finally reached my driveway, tired yet filled with true peace, encouragement, faith, and commitment. I gave thanks yet again, and went to bed that night with no idea of how my life would change in just a few months.

On Air

Jim Shorts here to set things straight.

Kevin is always talking to himself; you can tell because his lips are always moving. And who is he talking to? He looks like an idiot, and I don't like walking next to him in public. I also don't like that he is always helping charities, because they are a big scam.

I hear he is getting holy. This worries me because I'm afraid he will stop me from saying the F-word. Isn't that what makes me a man? I will have to say silly things like "stuff and nonsense" or "oh, gee whiz." In my house, we never went to church. We just watched *Davey and Goliath* on TV.

TWELVE

Bad News

During my thirty years of broadcasting, I have often been asked, "What is something that happened to you on air that you'll never forget?" People are thinking of the assassination of John F. Kennedy or the 9/11 attacks, as these are powerful events in time. My personal on-air moment happened a few months after my confession, in the fall of 2008.

It was a Tuesday morning at 7:16 EST. I suddenly could not move my right leg, and from my elbow to my fingers, my right arm became numb. The broadcast studio began to spin around, and at that moment my microphone was on, because I was having a conversation with my newsman, Ed Buchanan. I became silent. Ed finished his news, and I played a song, something I seldom did. Then I said to my audience, "It's seven thirty. We'll be right back after these messages."

I shut off the studio mikes and quickly turned down the monitors. The room became dead calm, silent. Ed looked at me with his arms wide in a gesture of confusion.

"What are we doing?" he asked. I looked at him with an expression of fear, knowing the commercials would soon end and I would need to be back on air.

"Ed, something's wrong. I can't move. I can't move my right leg and even my arm and hand are numb," I said calmly. "Am I having a stroke?"

I had often joked to my audience about how cool it would be to die on the air with my microphone open and my body crashing into studio racks, with all the horror of death as it actually happens. People would be listening in their cars, on their way to work, hearing the radio personality Kevin Matthews die on air. *It would be so cool*, I'd thought. It was just the idea of the news reports all saying, "He died on air doing Jimmy Shorts!" appealed to me: *Now, that's good radio, real theater of the mind, and talk about material for a best-of show! Did you hear the audio they used on Channel 8? That's him really dying on the air. Can I get a tape of that?* Life and death reduced to a bit or just another day at the office shows how little worth I gave them.

As I look back on that Tuesday morning, I feel sadness, because the great talker said nothing. He did not ask for help, or honestly inform his audience, or request that they call 911. He did not say, "Ed, take over. Call my wife, please, because I can't move." He did not even say, "Someone, please help me." Instead, he was funny and would be fine, would play more music than usual, finish the show, say nothing, and go home and tell no one anything. *There is a show to do tomorrow; it's only Tuesday. Don't scare your wife. It will be Friday soon and you can drive back to Chicago. Good luck driving.* No, I did not call a doctor. I did not call my wife, not wanting to alarm her. The entire office watched me stagger down the hallway and then return to work the next morning. I told Ed I was feeling better. "I'll see a doctor this weekend. I'm okay."

THIRTEEN

To the Doctor

It was November, and a dusting of snow covered the roadways. *Great driving conditions.* My leg felt like a thousand-pound cypress log that had been soaking for years in a Louisiana swamp. Finally I entered our downtown apartment and greeted my wife with, "Hi, Deb. I need to go to the emergency room. Something is wrong with my right foot and leg, and my hand and arm feel numb."

At Northwestern Memorial Hospital, the emergency room doctor who examined me just shook her head. "I don't know what to tell you, sir. You may want to call your family doctor." I left the hospital as it was beginning to snow. It was a Friday night in Chicago. How many great Friday nights had I celebrated in this wonderful city, party central? And now it was all I could do to flag down a cab and head back to our apartment. I was exhausted. I could hear the honking of cars, sirens thirty floors below on Michigan Avenue. I had nothing to say to my wife. "They have no idea; they treated me like a homeless man who had stumbled in off the street." But I had to find out what was happening to me, so the following morning I called my cardiologist, Dr. Carroll, a dear friend whom I'd had on the air many times. He would see me in his office that day. I could tell by his voice that he was worried. He knew me well and had examined me in the past—high blood pressure, poor diet. He knew the lifestyle I had led for too many years.

Dr. Carroll greeted me in the lobby of his office and immediately saw that I was having trouble with my right leg and foot. After checking my heart rate, he ran an EKG to see whether I had suffered a stroke or heart attack, which I had not.

"You're not working, that's for sure, until we find out what is going on with you," he said, searching for the phone number of one of his associates. "I want you to see a friend of mine. She is one of the best neurologists, but she's a ball-buster, Kev. You had better do what she says."

I drove to the western suburbs with my wife for an MRI with contrast. Lying in a coffin that made pounding noises, its cold metal an inch from my lips, I could not move anything or it would ruin the test. *I'll simply have to deal with this.* I began to pray the Our Father. Back home, I thought about the neurologist who would read the MRI. *What if she hates men? What if she's not a fan of mine and hates my radio show?* Deb and I just sat together, listening to the traffic below, looking at the lights near Grant Park, thousands of tiny white lights that outlined Lake Michigan. Snow blew around the window. Nothing to do except wait.

On Monday we braved the rush-hour traffic, arriving at the neurologist's office with time to spare, and sat in my truck for as long as possible just looking at one another. "You can do this," said my wife. I entered the lobby, filled out more forms, and took a seat. Men, women, babies, and white noise filled the room. I flipped through a magazine, not reading one word. The clock on the wall teased me by seeming to move backward. I could hear the gum in my mouth, and I was chewing to a Rolling Stones song, "Monkey Man."

"Kevin, the doctor will see you now." We were guided to her office. My wife and I were seated in two chairs that looked across from her desk, her empty seat. The assistant said that the doctor would be right in and left the office door open. My wife and I just looked at one another. She took my hand and squeezed it tight. "You will be okay." I wanted to swallow my gum. *What if she hates gum chewers?* I tucked the gum up into my cheek, and suddenly she entered.

In the whitest doctor's coat I had ever seen, she was tiny and well dressed and commanded attention. She was also hot. *Great! She is going to see me in my underpants. I want a guy, oh no.* She took her seat, introduced herself, and warmly gave us her neurological history. Within seconds I knew Dr. Carroll had been right: She was the best. "Here is what we found, Kevin."

She showed us the MRI of my brain. "See this? This is a mass about the size of a walnut in the left lower portion of your brain, and it may be a tumor. If it is a tumor, where it is located cannot be operated on, according to my husband, who is a brain surgeon. There is nothing we can do if it is." *Wow, I was just told that I am going to die.*

"It's going to be okay," I told Deb. "Don't cry, sweetheart." She sat in quiet horror. I felt a sense of peace as my wife and neurologist talked about the treatment that was to come, although their voices seemed distant—calm conversations at a lower volume, almost a slight echo. The room became just a space, a floating point in time. I felt concern, but no true fear of dying. I don't believe in death, but in life in the hereafter, and now with grace, I snapped back. I continued to hold Deb's hand firmly and listened to the evaluation: "We can schedule a brain biopsy, but can't do that procedure for at least ten days, so go home and prepare for the worst. In the meantime, I want to perform more tests, because I am not convinced that this is cancerous. But get ready; get your life in order."

So this is how I am going to die, a brain tumor! Suddenly I thought, *Jim Shorts, Devon, Darrnell, every voice in my head has brain cancer.* I could not believe how calm I was. I never thought I would be told how I was going to die. *Why am I so calm? My wife—I have to be strong for my wife and my kids. What will the trades say? God, I finally get to meet you. I hope you can forgive me.*

Deb and I left the doctor's office, and we held hands as we drove home. She is one of the strongest, most graceful, most comforting human beings I know. For her, the news that day was not about material things, such as selling a house, paying bills, a career change, or the radio industry; it was about time, reality, and family—a husband, a daughter, and a son. We began to plan how to tell the kids. That scared me, because I did not want to see them cry and filled with worry. The ride back to the city was silent, except that Deb kept saying, "We will get through this." I will never forget that day. We were returning to a time when we had nothing as a young married couple—just love, one another, our faith, and our family. I had ten days to prepare for a funeral, maybe cook my last Thanksgiving turkey, tell my boss and coworkers, and prepare for more tests.

I wanted this Thanksgiving to be special, to be with my children, my wife, together as a family. I love Thanksgiving. I love cooking the traditional feast, the good china and the smell of turkey and gravy coming from the kitchen, the sound of a football game in the other room and the laughs around the table. This would be a celebration of life, of giving thanks and looking into the eyes of my children and my wife. I would take it all in, remember it, not be afraid. But I was. I was terrified, not of dying, but of having a drill bit bore through my skull.

Okay, soon you're going to admit me into the hospital, drill a hole in my head, and then take a wire, enter the hole, puncture my brain, drive the probe deep into it and into what could be a tumor the size of a walnut, clip some tissue, grab it, and pull it out through the hole you just drilled. All of this, while I am awake?

I received a spinal *(wonderful!)*, had test after test, and gave gallons of blood, leaving my arms bruised like a heroin addict's. There were more MRIs and more pictures of my brain. The good news was that I had a brain, and it was not in my ass, as so many had said.

My neurologist began to look more closely at the white mass. It was the size of a walnut, but it also had two tiny horns on it.

"Look, Kevin. See those tiny strands on top of the mass? I've seen that before, rarely—but I've seen this type of growth before. It may be a huge scar; it may be multiple sclerosis!"

Okay, so her husband, the brain surgeon, is betting on a brain tumor, and she is pushing her chips all in, betting on multiple sclerosis to win. To prove it, she ordered me to undergo intravenous steroid treatments immediately. For the next ten days, I took the treatments and also oral steroids. I ate them like Tic Tacs. I was ordered to stop smoking, stop drinking alcohol, and eliminate sugar. Nothing I loved could be ingested—nothing. I was put on a low-calorie diet and was encouraged to drink water only. *How fun!*

The steroid treatments had me buzzing. I felt like an atomic volunteer who'd stood too close to the Nevada desert blast site during the early 1950s Cold War. Everything I loved to eat and drink was now forbidden, and if this steroid treatment didn't work, my doctor's husband would get to drill a hole in my head. *Perfect.*

I was admitted to the hospital and began filling out paperwork that would allow doctors to drill, ruining my beautiful head of hair. Sooner than I knew, I was sitting on a brain surgeon's examining table with Deb by my side, looking at outdated magazines. I was an hour away from having a brain biopsy. I was not worried about dying, but even the thought of having my head drilled hurt. I kept remembering the Three Stooges. How many times did Curly get his head drilled by Moe? *Calling Dr. Larry, calling Dr. Moe, calling Dr. Curly.* I had been told that once the hole had been drilled, I would not feel the probe entering my brain, because the brain is free of sensation, but moving the probe deep into my brain could leave me paralyzed, unable to talk, walk, or move again. *God help me. Please make that drilling not hurt.* Suddenly the waiting room door opened and in came my neurologist and her brain surgeon husband.

"I was right. It's not a brain tumor, and it is MS. That mass in your brain is a scar, a giant scar that we can treat. You have MS, Kevin." My wife and I stood up and started hugging and laughing. *It's not a tumor; it's MS. . . . What in the hell is MS?* I didn't even know how to say it. The room exploded in cheers; the thought of not having a hole drilled in my head gave me great joy. As we high-fived one another and everything slowly became silent, I asked the question.

"So what is MS? Is that bad?"

FOURTEEN

MS

The doctor explained to my wife and me that I had a rare type of multiple sclerosis, and that we would continue steroid treatment and begin MS treatment, which required me to inject myself daily. *Give myself a shot?* I hated shots. *Give myself a shot every day, for the rest of my life?* As we left the hospital, I knew I needed to return to Grand Rapids to host my morning show, and Deb and I decided that Chicago offered the best care for my disease, which has no cure. It was going to be back and forth.

My treatment began immediately: weeks of steroids, daily visits to the hospital, IVs, and later weeks of tablets by mouth. The walnut-size mass that was visible on the first MRI had not been reduced; my walk was still awkward, like Frankenstein's. I kept hearing Aerosmith's "Walk This Way" as I maneuvered with the physical therapists. My arm was still numb, as numb as it had been on that fateful Tuesday at 7:16 a.m. But I could return to work. My audience thought that I had taken time off to be with my family during Thanksgiving. I had told only family, close friends, and the station's general manager about my diagnosis. What was I going to tell my audience? I packed up my truck and headed east to Grand Rapids. I had a radio show to do, and it was the holidays, the most wonderful time of the year. Ho, ho, ho.

My morning show was now different. Whereas I usually stood behind the microphone, now I needed a chair. I
could no longer run into the newsroom, because my balance,
walk, and timing were off. I had trouble remembering guests'
names. Difficulty greeted me on my first day back on the air.

Fortunately, I was able to take time off for Christmas and
New Year's Eve, and my audience was distracted by the holidays. I was back, something had happened, but the holidays
had provided cover, a time not to be heard, not to be seen. I
had not told them why I had been missing; management had
felt uncomfortable about it because they feared a negative
reaction from listeners and advertisers.

I have always been honest with my audience, and so I was
not going to keep silent about this for long. I told the general manager that I wanted to hold a press conference and let
my audience, advertisers, friends, and the industry know the
truth. He was not thrilled that I was going public, but I knew
that I could never hide such news from my radio fans. We
were family, my audience and I, and we shared everything in
life—about our marriages, kids, life in general, and now mor-
tality. "I will not keep this a secret," I said.

So, on November 8, 2008, I sat in a crowded conference
room with news cameras, newspaper reporters, and television
anchors gathered, waiting for my statement and answers to
their questions: "Why were you gone so long?"

"Are you returning to Chicago?"

My general manager broke the ice: "Kevin has been

diagnosed with something. Here's Kev to tell you all." I had no notes. Like my comedy act, it would be just another stage with people in the crowd staring at me, ready to laugh, no cover charge, two-drink minimum, please tip your waitress. I was waiting for my wife to arrive, but she was running late because of winter weather.

"I have multiple dystrophy," I told the reporters, proof that I knew very little about this new beast called multiple sclerosis. *I'm dying. This set sucks—no laughs, and the room feels hot, crowded, and lifeless.*

Suddenly my smart, beautiful, and articulate wife entered the room, coming to my rescue. She looked stunning. She took the seat next to me, and my general manager introduced her to everyone. Pens, paper, and cameras were in hand, ready to report the big secret. She calmly took over the press conference and spoke about my condition with elegance and poise. The beautiful mother of our children and the stability of our household, Deb, a summa cum laude graduate of Loyola University, began:

"Kevin was diagnosed with a rare type of multiple sclerosis. His treatment will continue in Chicago . . ." And on she went, beautiful and to the point, my best friend, next to me, holding my hand, calmly telling the truth. Again as I had in the doctor's office, I floated above the crowd, hearing the echo of talk below. As soon as Deb said "multiple sclerosis," I came back to the room of reporters, and clarity replaced the reverb of noise.

"And now you know. That's the truth and life goes on," I said. But would it? The press left the conference, and within minutes Grand Rapids, Chicago, and the whole industry knew the big secret. Immediately the phones began to ring as the news was reported. It was all over Facebook and Twitter. The audience began to call my morning show, and so did my mother, my sister, my neighbor, my best friend, my brother, his wife, her husband—so many callers. Encouragement filled the airwaves. I would soon learn that at least one person listening to my weekly radio show would be diagnosed with multiple sclerosis every day. Support groups, wellness centers, and community leaders embraced my diagnosis with open arms, but how would this affect my ratings?

My radio audience appreciated my honesty and honored my wife, who had spoken so eloquently at the press gathering. We were now in this fight together: Listeners called—"My sister has MS"—and there were more calls, letters of support, charities who could help, and the suggestion of events we could have, while management seemed to move to a wait-and-see strategy.

The year 2009 had come in with a neurological bang. Looking back, the game had changed, and I was physically and mentally impaired. Suddenly all of my characters—Jim, Devon, Darrnell—had MS. I had never wanted to become a victim; instead I wanted to learn more about autoimmune disorders: *What could have caused this? Was it the water, or the wild golf outings? Did I contract something in Japan? Will I end up in a wheelchair?*

I came to the realization that I would never run again or play golf, as my balance and equilibrium were too far off. I loved sailing, but continuing to do that seemed impossible, too, and shooting shotguns was now too dangerous. I was thankful to be alive, though. *If the mass in my brain had been cancer,* I thought, *I would be dead by now.*

I transferred to doctors in Grand Rapids. The medical facilities there are some of the best in the world. I was introduced to a brilliant neurologist and became a patient at the Hauenstein Center. It was there that I continued treatment; I learned to inject myself daily with a medicine that simply kicked my ass, because there is a fatigue that comes with MS. This particular medication is brutal, and it can cause depression; the warning label even indicated, "Caution. May cause suicidal tendencies." *Yup, sure does.*

FIFTEEN

Dave Mason

In addition to fatigue, my balance and walking became a challenge. I was introducing the Rock and Roll Hall of Fame singer Dave Mason one evening when I found it nearly impossible to climb the stage stairs. Walking through the instruments was the biggest challenge, because I could easily have fallen into Dave's guitar or onto the drum rig. He just looked at me with an "Are you okay?" look. I felt the heat of the stage lights, and wondered for a minute who I was introducing. I finally brought out this musical legend, and my exit was just as slow as my entrance. No longer was I the star. This new sidekick, multiple sclerosis, was stealing my act.

The radio program limped along with my leg; my comedic timing slowed like a rusted clock. My treatment was a new routine that would continue for life, back and forth to Chicago, injecting myself with a needle every day. The injection sites—my butt, my stomach, under my arms, my legs—became sore and bruised. I was depressed and hollow-eyed, and death was a way out. My faith in Jesus is what kept me alive, and my wife and children. *Suicide is not a solution.* I kept thinking of my Navy SEAL friends: "Ring the bell. Pain is temporary; quitting is forever."

I was constantly talking to God, to Jesus: "What do I do with this, Jesus? What now?" Since the age of four I'd been

talking to him, lying in my bed, hearing the yelling downstairs; now decades later, I found myself comforted by God in
silence. I felt the presences of peace and patience and remembered what my Iroquois grandfather had said: "Death is just
a word, brother. Float like a feather. Try and out-give God,
Kevin, every day. Try and out-give God." This amazing man,
Sana, my grandpa. His presence was all around me. I could
smell him in the room, the smell of sage, just for a moment, as
a gentle reminder that there is no end. I had been fortunate to
have met many stewards of the earth, simple, loving, peaceful
elders, constant resources of hope and conduits to God.

And God and the elements had prepared me for this. I
thought back to the previous Good Friday, before MS. I had
sat alone at St. Anthony's, not praying, but listening intently
to the sounds around me: thunder, the rain on the church
roof, my breathing, the rhythm of my heart. I had felt as if I
were back in my tree stand in the woods, no humans around,
no sounds of humanity, just natural noises. I had known
then, without knowing anything specific, that something was
coming.

What was coming was a storm, just like the one pounding the church: black clouds, thousands of raindrops slamming into the metal roof. A friend's face had come to me,
eyes closed, in church, listening. Then his personal pain had
become more vivid. It was impacting me and those who knew
him and lived with him. This year I would be diagnosed with
MS. The following year, I would be unemployed, the scariest

year of my life. The dark storm that surrounded me in the church was warning me, telling me to get spiritually prepared, because something was coming, and it *did*.

All I could do was prioritize the most important aspects of my life: God, family, and work. I thought I was keeping these spinning and in order. We sold our home. Teage would be attending college, and Trevor was establishing a musical career. Deb and I were looking forward to moving to Grand Rapids, where we were married. But as I write these pages, I see that I was still placing work before God and family. Life continued: radio, treatment, blood tests, needles, MRIs, finding a house. *How's college going? Loved your last song, Trevor. Where did the summer, the fall go? What happened to 2008? It's already New Year's Eve 2009.*

SIXTEEN

Go to the Cemetery

It was St. Patrick's Day 2009 in Chicago, which celebrates the Irish in style with parades, drunkenness, and tradition, and by dyeing the Chicago River green. Everyone is Irish on St. Patrick's Day. I was in Chicago for treatment, and my wife and I were making final preparations to move her to Grand Rapids. Our home in the suburbs had sold, the Chicago apartment's lease was ending, and I was weaning myself from my neurologist to continue treatments in Grand Rapids. Finally, the brutal commutes were going to end.

I had just signed a new contract that I thought would provide stability, enabling me to buy my wife a house and to live with the challenges of MS happily ever after. I needed to visit an attorney in the western suburbs of Chicago. It was just after 9:00 a.m. when I left downtown. Normally I would take the Stevenson Expressway, but not today. The city was wall-to-wall Irish, and the roads throughout were closed. Floats were lining up for the big parade in three hours. Soldier Field, Grant Park, and Michigan Avenue were closed. The crowds were building by the thousands. How was I going to get out of Chicago?

It was a beautiful March day, not a cloud in the sky. This St. Patrick's Day was going to be well attended. The air was clean, and I could hear bagpipes, the sounds of the city, the crowds, through the windows of my truck as I slowly crept, block by block. I was escaping the city I loved, and during St. Patrick's Day, of all days.

I finally broke from the huge mass and reached Ohio Street. I knew the way by heart: Ohio to the Dan Ryan, to the Eisenhower Expressway, west to Wolf Road. As soon as I entered the Eisenhower Expressway, I had a sudden urge to go to the cemetery. I knew exactly which cemetery: Queen of Heaven, in Hillside. The Eisenhower Expressway was my path. I drove in silence and suddenly my attorney's appointment could wait. I felt such a desire to visit this special place, one of the oldest cemeteries in the Chicago area.

Queen of Heaven has an interesting history. In the early 1990s, people began to gather around a very old tree in the back of the cemetery. It had been hit by lighting, and the mark on the tree trunk resembled the Virgin Mary. Throughout the years, thousands had gathered to pray the Rosary there. Families brought their children, and many people had felt the presence of Mary. Even after vandals had destroyed the tree, so many people still came that the cemetery finally built a huge cross, depicting the Crucifixion, and placed it in a location that could accommodate the larger crowds.

As I drove west on the Eisenhower, my truck cab was silent—no radio, just silence on such a fine day. Through my sunroof, I could see the vibrant blue sky above me. It had been years since my wife, our children, and I had visited this place, this peaceful shrine, this holy land outside Chicago. Finally I saw the exit for Wolf Road. I took it south.

I turned into the main entrance to the cemetery, and it was as if I knew exactly where to go: down this road, now left, down a bit more, right, then another left, and straight ahead. There it was, a large circle of cement, and in the center a giant crucifix, Jesus hanging from the cross. I entered the parking lot and noticed an old van in one of the stalls. No one else was there; just a man sitting in a rusty van, looking at the cross. I parked at the other end, respecting his privacy. I sat for a moment, looking at the crucifix. I had two choices: Sit in the truck, or walk to the cross. I was embarrassed to walk to the cross, thinking that the man in the van might think I was crazy, or drunk because of my poorly functioning right leg and foot.

I quickly decided to leave the truck and walk to the cross, but I had nothing of spiritual importance on me. I did not have a cross around my neck, and I never wore my wedding ring, because I didn't like wearing jewelry of any kind. Looking up at my truck's sun visor, I discovered that I had been traveling with a brochure that my wife had picked up after visiting Fatima with her mother and sister-in-law not long ago. It was a small blue booklet, intended to protect me in my travels between Chicago and Grand Rapids. It had been responsible for thousands of miles of safety that I had forgotten. Now it was in my hand.

The brochure was titled "Our Lady of Fatima: Our Mother Comes to Us." With it in my numb right hand, I opened the truck door with my left. I did not care whether the man in the van thought I was crazy limping up to the crucifix. Like the woman in the Bible who touched the hem of Jesus, I simply wanted to touch his feet. I slowly walked to the cross with the Fatima brochure, reached above me, and placed my hand on Jesus' feet. The statue was so big that his feet were higher than my head. As soon as I touched them, I began to say the Lord's Prayer. I never took my hand with the brochure away. "Jesus, help me. I am so scared, so confused. Please be with me and my family." Tears filled my eyes.

As I continued to pray, I felt water dripping onto my hand, which I did not remove, but continued to press against his feet. It slowly ran from my fingers and down onto my wrist. A path of water was wrapping around my arm, and the numbness that I had known for months was gone. I could feel my hand again, and my arm. My arm, from the wrist to the elbow, worked!

I moved from the feet and began to rub the wetness on the back left side of my head, so that my dry hair now became damp. I took what was left and rubbed my leg, my blue jeans, with my wet hand. *I wish I could touch the skin*, I was thinking. I was standing at the cross. Jesus' two cement feet, a nail in each of them, and the cross were all I could see. I slowly looked up, and there were his legs, his torn wrap, his stomach and chest, whip lashes, and the mark of a sword. His head was down, tilted and looking at me. There were thorns, embedded into and circling his head.

I knew at that moment that Jesus Christ had never left me; I had left him, and now we were together again in a quiet cemetery on a beautiful St. Patrick's Day. The fear and confusion I had taken to the cross had been replaced by joy. I could feel my hand again. I could feel my arm. "Commit. Commit to whatever you have, to the burden of injections, to treatment. Commit to your children, to your wife. Commit to me."

I could not wait to tell my wife, who had visited this cemetery with my children and me. This time I had carried her Fatima brochure, and it had touched the feet of Christ of the crucifixion.

SEVENTEEN

Home from the Cemetery

My God, I've just witnessed a miracle, and it happened to me. As I turned to leave, I said one more prayer. Looking up at Jesus, I simply said, "Thank you. I love you so much." Once again, I moved my right hand, making what seemed like hundreds of fists, stretching my fingers apart. My hand and right arm had feeling; the numbness *was* gone. I wished that I could bathe in the water.

I turned and slowly walked back to my truck, holding the booklet from Fatima in my newly repaired right hand. I was hoping that the water I had rubbed on my head was healing the walnut-size growth located in my brain. *Believe* was the word running through my thoughts. *Believe.* I felt my hand and arm once again.

As I walked, I noticed the man in the van looking at me. *You should go and pray with him,* I kept thinking, but he was in his own circle and needed to go on his own.

I drove through the cemetery, looking at all the markers and headstones. *Are these people with Jesus? Did they witness what happened at the cross?* I finally reached the cemetery exit and drove to the appointment I had scheduled with my attorney. I had no desire to tell him what had happened; he is the kind of guy who would say, "Sure. Get out of here." I learned long ago from my Native American friends that not everyone is going to believe you. *Be careful who you tell.*

I drove in silence back to the city—no radio, windows up. For the first time since this circus had begun, I felt real peace. I had no fear of anything, but—as I think about it now—the darkest days were yet to come.

Looking back, I think the water that touched my hand and arm was another type of baptism. Coming from the feet of Jesus Christ, it reminded me that he has always been with me—not just since the age of four when I hid in my bed, scared of my dad, but since birth—and I had just had physical reassurance that each day forward I would never be alone. As I drove, I remembered the calm that had come to me on the day the doctor told me that I might have a brain tumor and that nothing could be done, that I should prepare to die. I never once asked God, "Why me?" I needed to comfort my wife and family, my friends and radio audience, but I never got mad or became a victim. I just asked, "What now, Jesus?" This question might take time to answer, but I knew that it had been answered at the foot of the cross, alone in a cemetery with a man in a rusty van watching, on St. Patrick's Day. It was then that I learned to trust God, his son, and Mary.

I burst through the apartment door and erupted in joy. "Deb, I can feel my right arm. Look! My hand works." I told my wife about my unexpected drive to the old cemetery, and she knew immediately which cemetery I was talking about. I told her what had happened. Confusing though it may have seemed, she believed me and could not help but notice my transformation. There was a joy, a new sense of relief and spiritual confidence. It is therapeutic to give your troubles to Jesus Christ. *Okay, I have MS. What do we do with it? How can we help others, especially young kids?*

I knew that it was important to move my wife to Michigan once our apartment lease had expired. I thought it would be fun to return to where it all began, where I had met Deb, where we got married, where our son was born. We found the perfect home just outside Grand Rapids in an area we have both loved since our college days, and we were soon living the country life. *Bye-bye, Michigan Avenue, with your traffic jams and high cost of living.* Now we found ourselves next to farms with cows and horses.

I needed to secure treatment for my MS. It is true that Chicago offers some of the best treatment in the world for neurological diseases, but Grand Rapids is also a leader in neurological care and treatment, and I soon met the most sincere doctor, a genius who would listen to me. I found immediate comfort, and I felt safe with a sense of hope. My new doctor loved jazz, the classics, Miles Davis, and Coltrane, so office visits became a relief. I was given choices of medications, including a recommendation of a less potent injection with fewer side effects that would alleviate fatigue and depression and afford better balance. My life was becoming stable because I had my wife at home, a great and caring doctor, a community, a church, and Father Mark, who was becoming not only a dear friend, but a spiritual mentor. It was he who had heard my confession, and my love for the Virgin Mary, the mother of Christ. I was becoming more involved in church and civic activities. I became a spokesperson for the Hauenstein Center, where I was being treated, creating jazz events that increased public awareness of the center.

Although my personal life was becoming stable, my radio career was not. For the next two years, beginning in 2008, the radio industry, as well as television and print media, was imploding, and it continues today. Media companies bought other media companies; the public bought stocks; stations cut staff, budgets, and marketing; high-profile, costly talent became expendable. Multiple sclerosis was a costly liability.

It was no secret that I could not perform as I once had. The heat from the broadcast equipment made standing during my program impossible, and I needed to sit, even though standing gave me more energy and greater access to the controls. My cognitive skills caused sometimes-awkward on-air conversations when I forgot what I was saying or who I was interviewing. At the same time, my responsibilities increased due to staff reduction and smaller budgets. Peer pressure, tension, and stress replaced purpose and love.

EIGHTEEN

The Rosary and
the Church

I found church and prayer comforting. Since my visit to the cemetery on St. Patrick's Day, I trusted God. Believe me, I worried, but I was finding peace in enjoying the real miracles around me: my children, hearing a new song from my son, cooking meals at church, attending chemo treatment with a teenager who faithfully listened to my radio program, meeting a kid with muscular dystrophy, and having lunch with a city leader with Parkinson's.

Since my confession, my love for the Virgin Mary seemed less shameful. I was never punished by God; rather, I began to see how I'd punished myself since birth. I was beginning to forgive myself and to understand that I have always been loved—and always will be loved—by God, by Jesus, by Mary, and by all above me. I had a great desire to understand the Rosary, admiring those who prayed it but never understanding the meaning of the beads. How beautiful they are: blue, white, deep red, held in the hand, lips moving. *What are they whispering?*

I am proud that I am an Irish Catholic. I remember watching my grandfather and grandmother, Gump and Maude, rock in big wooden rockers on a wooden porch, back and forth, holding their beads. My grandmother, her lips colored with a soft pink lipstick, would be whispering, talking to someone very important. I loved my grandfather, a big, barrel-chested Irish cop, who lived in Owasso, Michigan. From the age of three, I remember sitting on his lap; we would rock and rock, in the same chair where he would say the Rosary every day. His white dress shirt was always stained with faint yellow spills from gravy or corn. I watched Gump feed homeless people who knocked at his old screen door. He never turned away anyone. He called me "Keevin." It seemed to me that he could never say my name correctly. He was often distracted by so many grand-kids crawling on him, and his house was filled with noises—the stomping of feet, the sound of a lamp falling to the floor, screen doors slamming, pots and pans dropping on the linoleum. I loved him, and I watched him nightly say his prayers, stand, and take five aspirin, which he washed down with two fingers of Irish whiskey. My first life lesson given by this man: "Never be afraid of a man who hits a woman, because he is no man."

I was a young teenager when my grandfather died. I did not want to go to the funeral, because I wanted to remember him rocking me, smoking those cheap cigars; going to church every day, when he could still walk; and most of all, holding those blue beads, his mouth moving, no sound, just looking up into the sky. I would later learn it was God he was speaking with, and those beads were his rosary. Eventually I found my mother's rosary; I carried it in my pants pocket and prayed randomly with it.

Church was becoming more than just a building, and my relationship with Father Mark and those attending St. Anthony's was becoming one of family. Our culinary events of the past continued to raise much-needed money for the school and the church, but one year we needed a thousand dollars to reach our goal. So I was auctioned off. The gymnasium was packed and someone offered to pay a thousand if I would agree to be an altar boy for three Masses one Sunday. Within seconds hands began to raise. Sold for a thousand dollars! "Kevin Matthews, you are now an altar boy."

Months passed, and I knew that I had to fulfill my commitment to serve every Mass one Sunday. *Okay, I can do this.* Four young kids, third- and fourth-graders, met me before church. I was handed an adult white robe and placed it over my street clothes. I was to be the cross bearer, leading the group of boys and girls into church, followed by Father Mark. This was not embarrassing; it was important. I grasped the cross. The music was my cue, and I began to process, but the stress began to trigger my MS and I was losing my balance. *Please don't let me fall and drop the cross, please!* As I walked down the aisle, with four kids and a priest following me, the congregation began to notice me. I knew not everyone had been at the auction and imagined them thinking, "Who is that big, fat guy with the huge horse head?"

I made it to the altar, and Mass officially started. I placed the cross in its holder and staggered back to my tiny cohorts. Finally we sat, and I towered above them. I was afraid that someone was going to sneak out of church to call the police, as Father Mark did not address my freakish presence. But in the homily, he did a wonderful job of embarrassing me, and the church filled with laughter. As Mass continued, I found myself in a privileged spot next to the altar, just inches from Father Mark. The church looked different; I could see everyone. My biggest fear was of falling; the marble steps seemed like the edge of the Grand Canyon. I was glad not to be holding the cup or the Eucharist during Holy Communion, because the body and blood of Jesus Christ are sacred to me.

Serving during church made me so proud. As Father Mark performed the service, I began to pray, *God, let me work for you. If I work for you, you will never fire me. I won't have to worry about ratings. I will never be unemployed; the job lasts for eternity.* I truly said those words while working as an altar boy. From that moment, I felt a devotion to Christ I'd never felt before, one that had begun at the auction months earlier. It became vividly clear to me that nothing is a coincidence.

I have photos of the end of Mass, with me carrying the cross to the back of the church, surrounded by kids who came up to my knees. It was fun serving Mass, but I was most aware of the peace that had come to me when I asked God to let me work for him. No more radio—I wanted a job that lasts for eternity. Little did I know that my wish was about to come true, for soon I would be fired from radio, most likely never to return.

PART II

Broken Mary

NINETEEN

Finding Mary

In the fall of 2011, after days of wind and rain, I decided to take a ride in my Ford truck to see the red and orange leaves, remember bowhunting days, and just be quiet. I love this time of year, and so as I drove along, I thought of days upon days deep in the forest, up in a tree, just listening and watching carefully in absolute silence. On the whole earth, the woods are my favorite place.

Slowly, with the warmth through the sunroof on my shoulders and Nicotine gum in my mouth, I moved my right foot to the accelerator. It felt numb, like I was wearing a hundred-pound ski boot. *This is not good,* I thought. *How long will I be able to drive?* And I cherished the moment all the more. It was quiet, windows up, no radio, the traffic moving in unison down Cascade Road. So I began to talk to one of the voices of those friends that Mom had known about years ago. This particular monotone I had heard before, but not often. It was comforting and spoke to me differently than the others, making me pay attention—very close attention, like a silent bank alarm alerting only those who need to know.

Go to the store you visited with Deb and buy her some flowers.

I had planned to pick up barbecue supplies at Lowe's, but buying a gift would be a nice gesture for my wife. *She's been busy lately,* I thought, *and flowers will make her smile.* The voice challenged me, and I had learned to trust it, to follow it and listen carefully; so I drove directly to the flower shop. It was trendy and expensive—not the kind I would usually patronize. Noticing that I was the only one in the lot, I parked directly in front of the door. The shop seemed empty. *What if they're closed?* When I got out of the truck and started toward the front door, I heard, *Look toward the dumpster.* I moved in the direction of a blue metal dumpster set against the side of the shop. It was not full, and the plastic lid fit perfectly.

Look down. Without hesitation, I glanced between the outside wall of the shop and the dumpster, and there, lying in the weeds and loose garbage, was a three-foot statue, broken cleanly in half. It was a most beautiful Virgin Mary, on her back with unspeaking lips and dark eyes gazing at heaven. She looked so helpless and cold, surrounded by pop cans and old papers, with dirt and dead leaves as her bed. Her praying hands were badly damaged; she had no fingers. Yet she seemed silently in prayer.

Take her from here. She doesn't belong here; do not leave without her. Take her home. The sense of duty did not scare me, but rather directed me as I stood above the broken statue of the blessed mother of Jesus littered with trash, tired and helpless. I felt an immediate sadness, yet I was inspired by courage and confidence. I would take her home. *How hard could it be to remove this statue? No one wants her; she's been thrown away.*

"I'll be back, Mary," I said to the empty air. "I'll bring you home with me and take care of you." I headed toward the door, the tinkle of bells announcing my entry into the shop. "You have a customer," they said. *I want to buy something,* I mused, *but not here in this store. I want a treasure that you have thrown away, the mother of Christ. Jesus, I promise to protect and care for your mother.*

As the door closed behind me, I heard the pleasant bells again, but I would soon compare them to the clang of ringside. Round one was beginning, and I would discover that the fight had just begun. I would go the distance and take on the challenge, and I was sure that the Holy Spirit was in my corner.

The empty store smelled of flowers and fertilizer. There were pots for planting, dried sticks twisted to hold fall flowers, and big stones that read, WELCOME, LOVE, and PEACE. I moved to the front counter, near a stack of papers for wrapping bouquets. Rose stems lay scattered to the left of a cash register. Flowers in buckets, flowers in glass vases, and flowers ready for delivery stood on a long table in the back. All was silent, just like my truck. *I've had enough silence,* I thought. Who works here?

"How may I help you?" I was startled by the shuffle of a clerk moving to my left to stand in front of the register. *I don't know how to put this,* I thought. *It better be good.*

"I'd like to have that broken statue of Mary outside next to the dumpster," I stated bluntly. The woman looked puzzled; confused by my request, she made busy motions.

"What statue?" she barked. I politely began to describe the Virgin Mary lying outside, broken in half, next to the dump-

ster. She paused, and her eyes began to close. She was thinking, translating my words, trying to understand.

"Oh, that. That's not for sale. It's a family heirloom," she
said offhandedly. It wasn't logical—why would a family heirloom be lying next to the dumpster?

*Uh-oh, here we go. God help me. Jesus, your mom's in the trash
outside,* I said to myself. The clerk was becoming agitated, her
silence tangible, her eyes closing, her lips pressing tightly together as if to shut off any possibility of trade or barter. She
seemed to be telegraphing, "Buy something or get out. You are
wasting my time, sir."

Dead air filled the room. In the silence, I said the fastest
prayer ever. In fact, the last time I had prayed so hastily I was
a hungry kid at Thanksgiving dinner, my stomach growling
and my favorite food just inches away. Now my quick and ur-
gent prayer was, *Jesus, what do I say? Help me now, please.* I broke
the silence with a peaceful suggestion.

"I will donate money to the Franciscans nearby in your
honor, for this shop, if you let me take that statue of Mary."

"Are you that guy on the radio?" she asked with a slow
smile and head tilted, recognizing my voice.

"Yes," I said. "I'm Kevin Matthews."

"I thought so. I listen to you every morning. Wow, I can't
believe you're here."

I thanked her for listening. *Whatever it takes to rescue Mary,*
I laughed to myself.

"I know some Franciscan sisters just north of town. I will give them money on behalf of you and the store, if you let me take Mary."

"Okay, sure. Take it," she said, suddenly changing her tune.

I stood in grateful silence. This felt like a spiritual black ops mission. I had won. Target secure. Mary was just minutes away from being transported to a safe zone. But now I was committed to giving money to a group of Franciscan sisters I barely knew. *How much must I donate? My daughter's wedding is coming up.*

Wanting to leave quickly, I thanked the clerk. As I opened the door, I heard the bell again and felt like Jimmy Stewart in *It's a Wonderful Life:* Whenever an angel gets its wings, a bell rings. I certainly had not earned any wings, but I had committed to a bunch of Franciscan sisters who would play an important role in my journey.

TWENTY

Broken Mary

Outside, I had time to see just how broken and neglected Mary was. *Why would anyone do this to an icon so beautiful, so holy?* Her gentle eyes seemed to stare at me. She must have been lying on this dirty piece of ground forever with her body broken in half at the waist. I looked again at the spot where her praying hands had been. Something must have sheared them off; they were now just stubs of gray concrete. She was covered in dirt, her paint faded in the front. The paint covering her back was much brighter, proof she had not been moved in a long time. Such a treasure just lying outside next to a filthy dumpster and a brick wall.

I picked up Mary's lower half and suddenly realized that the task was not going to be so easy; she was solid concrete. *This is a good twenty-five pounds*, I thought as I tried to get a grip on her. What a challenge! Because of my MS, moving the pieces was shaping up to be nearly impossible. The last thing I wanted to do, though, was return to the shop for help and risk a change of heart. Mary might be doomed to lie next to the dumpster for years. She needed to come home with me.

I learned long ago that you never talk about a woman's weight, but here lay Mary broken in two with each section weighing at least twenty-five pounds. I thought, *How am I going to lift these two pieces, walk over, and carefully place her in the back of my truck? My walk is now staggered, I have very little balance left, and it is difficult to lift anything over ten pounds.* I had no other choice but to ask for help: "God, please help me do this. Help me pick these pieces up and walk them to my truck. Please, God, help me."

I lifted the first piece, her feet. I noticed them standing on a rock, with red roses covering them. She stood on a snake, crushing it. The roses, not the snake, caught my eye, and her blue-and-white dress, chipped and so dirty. I just wanted to wash her. Such a beautiful woman, broken completely in two.

"One, two, three." I was lifting with my legs and not my back, my feet grounded. Even with weak shoulders, I raised her up in one motion, just as my high school gym teacher had taught me to lift weights. Although I had thought him a total jackass then, now his basic training was helping me carry Mary. It took all my concentration.

One of my favorite T-shirts reads, I AM NOT DRUNK. I HAVE MS. I must have looked like Frankenstein walking with the heavy pieces of Mary, or Cuba Gooding Jr. being ordered by Robert De Niro to walk in *Men of Honor:* "I want my steps, Cookie. Walk to me, Cookie. Now! That's an order! You hear me, Cookie? I say, 'Walk!'"

I gently laid both halves of Mary on a moving blanket that I had in my truck. Looking at mine, her eyes seemed tired. Her paint was dirty; large chips dotted her body. What a beautiful piece of art! How graceful she must have been! I remember folding the blanket in two, giving Mary a more comfortable ride home. She was never a statue to me; she was a living human being.

"Let's go home, Mary. I'll take care of you from here on out." My eyes filled with tears and my heart with sadness. *Who could do such a thing to such a wonderful mother, to Our Lady, to our example of prayer?*

I drove home carefully, avoiding any bumps in the road; I did not want Mary to suffer any more breakage. I turned up the heat in my truck, because I thought that she must be cold from lying so long outside in the rain and wind. I felt I'd never seen anything so lovely, yet so broken. My truck was an ambulance—no sirens, no radio, just warmth and silence. Mary and me, driving to her new home.

At first the ride seemed awkward, because I did not know what to say. If you have ever traveled in a car with someone new, trying to make small talk feels strained. I certainly knew who she was, but in my truck, driving on a fall day in Michigan, I didn't know how to begin. I broke the silence. "I am taking you home, Mary. You're safe now. I can't wait for you to meet my wife. She's a big fan of yours and loves you very much. I know a priest, too, whose name is Father Mark. I promise we will get you fixed. I promise."

As I drove up my driveway, I hit the garage door opener, and its sound was the loudest noise I had heard during the trip. *This noise is going to wake Mary.* It was a fear that I had experienced in the car with my children as sleeping babies.

I opened the back of the truck, and there was Mary

staring directly at the ceiling. She looked peaceful, so I took more blankets and made a comfortable, soft bed on a shelf. I laid both sections of her on the shelf as best I could, carefully piecing her together with a pillow for her head, making sure her feet were covered. Placing my right hand on her shoulder, I prayed a Hail Mary, promising to put her together again, and telling her to rest. My eyes became wet with tears. The Holy Mother is here, resting in my garage.

At that moment I knew that I had done the best that I could, and that Mary appreciated it, but a long, icy winter was coming, and walking with two heavy pieces would not be safe. I had no choice but to wait until spring, when life would return to earth. I remembered Sana, my wise Iroquois grandfather, who had taught me to pray outside and hear the silence of life in snow: "The earth is sleeping, but hears you," he would say. I would wake Mary in the spring.

"I love you and you are home, Mary. It will be okay now," I said out loud, seeing her for the first time as Broken Mary— like me, broken from MS, with so much of my life broken. But I knew that she would change me. I quietly walked away, almost tiptoeing to the back door, and entered the house. My wife was in the kitchen, and I spoke to her almost with a whisper, "Deb, come see what I found."

We walked back to the garage to the bed I had made.

"Look, it's Mary." We both kept silent. Then I motioned to return to the kitchen and the garage became dark and quiet, a resting place for this beautiful Mary, the mother of Jesus.

On Air

Jim Shorts here, getting shorter and shorter.

Kevin says Jesus is his best friend, and he loves Mary, but what about me?

This is why I hate Kevin.

TWENTY-ONE

A Circle

I remember a day in Chicago in 1995 when a Native American medicine man from Utah, a Ute, took me to a park. We were both sitting on the ground, and he told me to stand up.

"Now, put your arms out straight. Keep them stretched out and slowly turn your body and your arms around in a full circle." Conscious that we were in public and people were watching, I felt like a fool. I imagined the people thinking, *Is that Kevin Matthews? What is he doing with that weird Indian guy?* But I put my arms out anyway.

Standing in the park, I slowly began to turn, until I was back where I began. I stopped with my arms still extended, with the medicine man sitting on the ground looking up at me. He began to nod.

"That is your circle of life. Anything you bring into that circle is your responsibility. It is better to say no than to say yes to everything."

I was listening.

"If anyone or anything enters your circle, you have allowed them in, and now you must be responsible."

Decades later, as I write this chapter, calm in my silent studio, sipping coffee, hearing my jaw crack as I mash my first piece of Nicorette gum of the day, hoping that my editor, who is helping me tell this story of Broken Mary, my life's journey, understands—hoping my reader understands—I can see my circle starting to make sense.

This story, my story that began when I was four years old, crying alone, wishing someone in heaven would hear me, walk with me, and protect me during the decades to come, needs the Holy Spirit's guidance as I write.

I left the park that day with the medicine man, thinking of what was living in my circle of life. *Why did I stand up and do that?* I recalled everything in my circle: what I have collected since I was a baby boy, Rochester, high school, my first job, college, meeting my wife, marriage, radio, moving, St. Louis, Chicago, my children, jerks, friends, no private life. My circle was like a storage unit, packed from top to bottom. Nothing more could possibility fit. Mice, ants, and spiders had no room to move.

I treated my faith gingerly while broadcasting, but I raised my children in the Church and supported many Catholic charities during my career in Chicago. I was proud of my Notre Dame heritage: My second cousin was Father John Cavanaugh, president of Notre Dame. He buried President Kennedy, and buildings are named after him. But witnessing to the faith was difficult in the radio industry, which discouraged talking about religion and faith on air. It was fine to play "Shout at the Devil," but lay off the Jesus-think, the Catholic stuff—unless, of course, you could help get Notre Dame football rights.

Who was in my circle? My radio audience knew exactly

who I was and I sure did know my audience; we did everything together. We got married together; gave birth to children together; partied and laughed together; cried together when rock stars died, friends died, fads died. We lived together for decades and challenged authority, management, the guys who wore suits and ties, stupid program directors, consultants—anything considered normal.

I sponsored golf outings for Father Smith in Chicago. I hung out with Native Americans. My audience knew Ted Nugent and shotguns, bowhunted black bears, listened to me playing Frank Zappa while I said anything I wanted. My audience and I—we were in this rampage together. They knew I was a "wind talker." Sana, my Iroquois Grandpa, had said to me many times, "You talk into the wind, through that microphone. Laughter is good medicine. Do good. Reach as many as you can. Try and out-give God. Give thanks on air, and be proud of your Creator God, as he is proud of you."

Looking back, I had let defiance into my circle. For nearly a year and a half, while hosting the morning show at ABC, I'd had had the highest-rated program for men age twenty-five to fifty-four, with bonus checks to prove it, and then I was told the program director and general manager wanted to see me. I had sat down while the program director sat behind his desk with the general manager standing to my left.

"You're fired," he had said to me. "We are not renewing your contract. Thank you, but we are changing formats and our consultants want us to go younger. Turn in your key and pass, and leave the building. We will pack up your belongings and ship them to you."

I've had to tell my wife, Deb, three times in my life that I just got fired. She is a saint, strong and faithful. *Batten down the hatches. Lock and load. Here comes the storm.* My first was in St. Louis. That gig had lasted nine long months. But St. Louis led to Chicago, where history would be made, until talk was replaced by ESPN sports. My firing at ABC took me to CBS, where I had walked away from a pay cut, deciding to return to Michigan and start over where it all began. My five-year run in Michigan would also eventually come to a halt after a company buyout, budget cuts, layoffs, downsizing, and the revolution of the Internet.

But here I was, without a job, diagnosed with MS and now type 2 diabetes. No more golf for me; no more running; poor balance meant no more sailing or boating, no hunting. Yup, my professional life certainly had come to a halt.

What I did have was faith in God, a loving wife and two wonderful children, my big sister, and some dear, dear friends who had loved me before radio stardom and fame. My biggest support came from Father Mark and my church, St. Anthony of Padua. I also had a broken statue of the Virgin Mary in my garage, where she had been resting since the fall of 2011. How peaceful my garage had become during her rest! I caught myself many times just standing over her, praying, not with despair, but feeling a sense of peace and calm.

My faith was keeping me sane. Without it, especially during these hardest of times, I could have easily ended my life with a shotgun; drunk myself to death; or simply jumped in my SUV, left for the mountains of Wyoming, and run away forever. But my faith was forcing me to hear the Spirit, and—for once—stop listening to the voices in my head, those famous characters: Jim Shorts, Devon, Darrnell, Cliff Dic. An arena of voices were now unemployed; fade to black, end scene.

For the first time in my life, I needed to rest—not only slow down, but shut it all down, stop entirely. I felt like I was living on a cruise ship, pitching back and forth, with weakened cognitive skills and a daily challenged memory. Yet my faith was becoming stronger.

Maybe my circle of life was becoming smaller. What needed to be in my circle was now there; what needed to leave had left. If you want to know who your real friends are, lose your job and your popularity. Suddenly those people who always called you for free concert tickets and free plugs on the radio stop calling. Your cell phone stops vibrating, and you are alone. Those around you now simply love you for who you are. For them, it was never about fame or fortune. My circle was now much smaller, and that felt sad at times, and terribly lonely, and scary. But more often it felt good; it felt real. And it's felt real ever since I found the Virgin Mary lying next to a dumpster, whom I chose to bring into my circle. Something had told me to bring her home to rest, and I knew I had to put her back together again, and put myself back together, too.

TWENTY-TWO

Putting Mary Together

I keep wondering, *Why me?* I scare myself often, afraid that such a question will end the miracles this broken statue has brought to so many. I often feel ashamed and not worthy of being with such a sacred object, and the silent presence of Christ.

I never intended to write a book when I found Mary that day. I simply knew that I could not leave her broken in half in the dirt, looking up at the sky, covered in garbage, alone, next to a dumpster. I had found the statue in the fall of 2010, taken her home, and placed her carefully on a shelf in my garage, wrapped in warm blankets. The shelf was next to my truck, so each morning when I left for the radio station, I could not help but see her. She seemed to be resting comfortably, and often I would stop, gently placing my hand on her as I said a morning prayer, then jump into my truck and begin the day. I had left her on the shelf knowing that I would put her together in the spring. How, I had no idea, but she needed to be put back together again after the winter had gone. Without the snow, I could safely place her in my truck and drive to get her fixed.

Spring did come, the snow was melting, and I knew it was time to mend Mary. I had told Father Mark about finding her months before, so he knew that I had her wrapped in my garage, resting comfortably, and that I intended to put her together again.

"Father, do you know of any business that could fix this statue?"

"I do." And he gave me the name of a monument company on the west side of Grand Rapids. The following day I carefully placed the two pieces of Mary in my truck. Once again I wrapped her carefully for the ride and said a Hail Mary. I remember I did not turn on the radio, because I wanted total silence. I was careful driving that day, slow to avoid bumps and sharp turns. I talked to Mary from the front seat: "Don't worry. I am going to get you fixed and put you back together again. Are you okay?"

I am proud of my driving record. I have never been in a car accident since receiving my first driver's license decades ago; however, I get lost easily, especially on the west side of Grand Rapids. I seemed to be driving in slow circles, looking for the address Father had given me. I remember pulling off the road often. *Where am I? All I can see are cornfields, abandoned buildings, and mud.* I drove like a postman searching for a hidden mailbox. Cars and traffic passed me at high speed. I can only imagine what names I was being called, but I was determined to find the repair shop for broken statues and tombstones.

"Mary, where am I? Can you help me, please? I am lost."
Here I am, lost and asking directions of a woman who is broken in two, wrapped in blankets, and riding in the back. If the cops pull me over, imagine what they would think if they saw me talking.

Finally, after miles, I saw the sign and piles of gravel, cement mixers, cinder blocks, cement benches, and freshly made Mary statues. I could tell that the business had been there for years. I parked my truck and walked down a very steep driveway, patches of ice making for a cautious walk. I saw no one. Eventually I found myself standing before a huge pole barn. The giant aluminum door was open. Stones of all sizes and shapes covered the floor.

"Hello? Anyone here?" I calmly called. The air was cold and my leather jacket wasn't warm enough. I was worrying about how I was going to climb the steep driveway to return to my truck without falling. MS accentuates the importance of escape routes and paths of least resistance.

"Hello? Is anyone here?" I heard a door open way in the back of the building and saw the shadow of a man walking toward me.

"Can I help you?" he asked. We shook hands and I introduced myself, mentioning Father Mark. He knew who I was, and told me that he listened every morning. He wondered whether Jim Shorts was with me.

"Jim is at the office," I said, "but wait until you see what I have wrapped in my truck." We began walking uphill toward my truck, and he could not help but notice my awkward march.

"How is your MS?" he asked.

"Wonderful. Walking on ice is so much fun," I said with a laugh. I opened the back of my truck, and he saw Mary. I explained that I had found her next to a dumpster, and began to remove the blanket that covered her. He saw that she was in two pieces. I lowered the bottom half to the ground. I then moved her upper torso so that he could see her better. I had never washed Mary, so her chipped body was dirty. Although her praying hands were gone, her paint was faded, and pieces of cement were missing from her gown, her eyes gazed at the man, and her face and lips were undamaged.

"Can you put her top and bottom together, put her together again?" I asked.

He replied that he could, telling me how he could drill a hole, place a rod into her base, and never again would she come apart.

"I can make her brand-new. We can replace her broken hands, paint her from head to toe, make her perfect again, and no one will ever know she was so broken," he claimed. I stood looking at Mary on this gray day, with clouds covering the sky and wind beginning to fill the property. It was getting colder. I paused. *God, what do I do?*

"No," I said. "Let's put her back together, but leave the other damage. She represents all of us. We are all broken in some way."

He simply said, "Okay."

He continued, "I can put her back together so she is in one piece, and get this done within a week, if you want to pick her up then." We shook hands and said we would see each other in church that coming weekend. We carefully placed Mary on the floor of the garage. I stood over her face and told her I would be back. Her eyes and gentle smile looked content. I opened my truck door, sat, and rolled the window down.

"I'll be listening tomorrow," said my new friend. As I drove away, I felt sad that Mary was alone, lying on a wooden pallet. Then behind me, I saw two men take a portion of her broken body into a giant stone workshop, one with her upper body, the other with her lower. I trusted the two men. The truck seemed empty. *Please, God, watch over her.* I left to the sound of a gravel driveway under a gray sky. I had no idea where I was, lost on the west side, my driving companion, whom I had named Broken Mary, gone.

TWENTY-THREE

Trust Me

So much had happened since I'd returned to Michigan. I had buried my mother. My son, living in Hollywood, was working hard as a professional singer-songwriter, and my daughter was planning her wedding. Deb and I had bought a home. My father was growing old, and with his past haunting many, I was his only caretaker. Although I felt like a junkie, shooting up MS medicines each day, I continued to make listeners laugh, to make the station money, to think up new ideas, and to stay relevant in an industry that was sinking, but my profession was sailing through the perfect storm.

There was a rumor throughout the industry that the company I was working for at WLAV Grand Rapids was about to be captured by the second-biggest media monopoly in existence. The radio hurricane was near. A veteran like me simply raised the stock share value to the crest. I was the ship's commodity; a pork belly; cattle, corn, and soybeans. Buy, sell, and cash out. My contract was about to expire and I was assured of renewal, so a five-year contract was drafted, and I was told, "Trust me." For decades I had used the same attorney; he had drafted all of my contracts. My wife and I signed our new five-year deal in our newly purchased, empty house, the moving trucks still en route.

"Trust me," said the radio official. "We have to get this contract to New York today. No time for your attorney to read the small print. Trust me. Sign it. We need to mail your contract to corporate *today*." Little did we know that we were in the eye of the hurricane, still navigating the worst media storm. The biggest wave came crashing in, sinking my radio ship forever. The fine print read, "If our company is bought, this contract is null and void." Trust me.

It actually happened like this. I had just finished my morning radio program when I was told that the new boss would like to see me. When I entered his office, I saw two employees standing silent, hands folded, with flushed faces and eyes glued to the floor. I sat across from a man in a cheap suit with a baked-ham head and yellow teeth, and I could not help but notice his greasy hair. The rumors were true: Our company had been purchased, and my radio ship had been boarded by a thieving pirate, but instead of wearing a black bandanna, he had a comb-over.

"I am a really big fan, and loved hearing you on WLS AM in Chicago."

"I never worked on WLS AM."

"Yes, you did."

"No, I never worked on WLS AM 89."

"Whatever, we no longer will be needing your services. Today was your last show. We will pack up your office, send your belongings to your new address, and here is two weeks' severance pay." So much for "Trust me." I was one of eight employees fired that morning. As I left the pirate's office, I passed a line of human beings, waiting, teary-eyed, ready to walk the plank.

I drove home deeply troubled. *What now, God?* I opened the door to our new home and walked down the hallway to Deb's bathroom. She was just putting on her makeup, when I once again said, "I've been fired." She is an incredible woman, a gentle mother, and she has been a remarkable wife—traits I have taken for granted for years. I was the clown who made people laugh. I loved my kids and acted like a kid. I never grew up, but my wife brought loving maturity to our marriage. Decades earlier, she had known that storms would lie ahead and had prepared for the perfect storm. My family immediately rallied around me.

The news of my firing spread throughout the industry, and trade publications exploded: MATTHEWS FIRED. WILL MATTHEWS RETURN TO CHICAGO? MATTHEWS DYING FROM MS. MATTHEWS SUCKS. Calmly, Deb held my hand and took charge. I worried about house payments, car payments, lack of insurance—my MS medicine alone is eight thousand dollars a month—the stress, relapse. *Who wants to hire a cripple?*

I was totally broken, just like the statue I had dropped off last spring. All I had now was faith in God, my wife, and my family. *God, help me, please. I give you myself and this mess. You are the one I trust.*

All of this was happening before Christmas, the birth of Jesus Christ, delivered of his mother Mary, who is glorified through prayer. Millions of statues have been made in her image. One, in particular, was being repaired and would change many lives, including mine.

TWENTY-FOUR

Are You Listening?

Looking back, I truly thought my life, my career, was completely gone. I had lost my job; one doctor had said I had MS; another diagnosed me with type two diabetes. *How am I going to pay the bills, eat, and keep my house, my wife, my family?* But then I simply prayed to Jesus, "Help me. I am so scared and feel alone. Help me, Jesus, please. I give you my MS; I give you my bank account, my failing career, every mess, every sin, all this garbage, I give to you."

Everyone should read his or her Book of Life backward: Start from the very last page, the most recent day of your life, and begin to read toward the front, your very first page, your birth. What happened to you yesterday is a page in your book. What you are doing right now, reading this book about Broken Mary, its being recorded. Every moment, every action, every word is written for you to consider and perhaps enjoy later.

So let me look back. It was the spring of 2012 and Broken Mary had been put back together. She had not yet gone to hospitals, hospice centers, or the church she now calls home, but she had been blessed by Father Mark. She was gracing my dining room, next to the fireplace, for all to see. Each morning, I would sit and have my first cup of coffee with her. I would look over and see her hands without fingers folded in prayer, eyes looking up and at me, her smile soft and warm.

"Good morning, Mary. How are you today? I love you," I'd say, and my wife greeted her daily with "Good morning, Broken Mary. How are you?" It was a kind of morning offering, but it wasn't enough. I had been hearing and feeling a thought in my heart: *The Rosary; commit to the unborn.* And I remembered a Cherokee grandmother's advice: "Kevin, if you pick up one stone, just moving it will change the universe forever." I told Father Mark I was going to begin saying the Rosary every day during Lent. He smiled and said, "Good."

Okay, you have just made a serious Lenten promise. There was a problem: I didn't know how to say the Rosary. Yes, I am a Catholic, but like many, I was not up-to-date on my spiritual practices. *Where are the instructions? How do you work this thing?*

On the first day of Lent, I saw Broken Mary out of the corner of my eye, hands folded, smiling.

"Okay, Mary. What do I do?" I did the logical thing: I googled "how to say the Rosary." Suddenly sites appeared. *Which one is the best? How am I going to hold the rosary while reading the tiny print: Say this prayer, followed by that, now this. You're not on the right bead; start again.* Finally I found a site that offered audio, so I could listen and pray along.

So every morning I opened the Rosary site, prayed, then had coffee. I never drank coffee during the Rosary; only after as a caffeine reward for my accomplishment. Day by day, I prayed while listening to a man saying the Rosary, and I quickly began to understand the mechanics. Because each day of the week has different mysteries, it was a challenge to make sure I was hearing the correct prayer for that day on the audio site.

Good site, but I can do better. After all, I am a professional broadcaster with good pipes and a smooth sound. Something to think about for later.

I only missed reciting the Rosary once, but I did say it on the day after Lent, on the forty-first day. I simply forgot. Normally, I would have been hard on myself: *You failed. You missed a day. Forget about Lent, and do it next year.* Not this Lent. So I missed a day. I looked at the statue of Mary, silently said, "I am sorry," and then simply smiled to myself. *It's okay. Just do an extra one on the day after Lent.*

On Good Friday, I knew I had to say the final Rosary in church. Again, I heard in my heart, *Are you going to deny my mother?* I knew what to do. Before Mass, as people gathered, I needed to kneel publicly at the statue of Mary located in the back of our church. She is as tall as a real woman, with hands reaching out, palms up, and eyes looking down. She is clean, beautiful, with not one chip, and no dirt, just a beautiful statue of Our Blessed Mother. Someone had gently placed a wreath of flowers on her head and a large rosary around her neck. The ceiling lights highlighted her face and body. Her beauty and calmness radiated from this holy stone monument that represented the Holy Virgin Mary, and she was there with me.

This could be embarrassing. I knew that I had to say my last Rosary, not in an empty church, but in a crowded church. It was important that I did not hide my love for Mary. *Be proud; show love and respect to her. She, too, is your mother, as she is the mother of all.*

There I was, standing in front of this beautiful statue for all those gathering to see, and now it was time to kneel. Earlier that winter, I'd had my knee replaced. That and my MS were going to make kneeling a challenge. *What if I don't finish in front of all these people? Mary, Jesus, please help me to do this.* Soon I was kneeling, with no pain. I closed my eyes and saw no people. I began to pray the Rosary, and the church noise turned to silence. Within forty days, I had learned how to pray the Rosary without prompting, each bead, fingers moving forward, slowly, prayer after prayer after prayer. Then, finally, the Sign of the Cross. On the last day of Lent, my days of just reciting the Rosary were over, because I was beginning to pray.

When I stood up, my knee, which hadn't hurt during prayer, felt like it had been shot by a musket—back to reality. I was proud of what I had done. I finished and limped back to my pew, giving thanks and recalling that Jesus' pain on this day more than two millennia ago was much worse than mine, and he had done it for my sins, our sins, because we are broken; we are loved but broken, children of God, wanting to be repaired.

TWENTY-FIVE

Traveling Mary

Things began to happen for Broken Mary. As soon as I'd had the statue put together again, she came alive, touching and changing not only my life, but so many others as well.

I was invited by Father Mark to speak about Broken Mary at church on Sunday after his homily. Without thinking, I said, "Yes, sure." And before I knew it, I was slated to speak to the entire church, every Mass. *What have I gotten myself into? This is not a comedy club. Help me, Jesus. Code red.*

I brought the statue with me on a carrying cart and placed her in the sanctuary covered with a white sheet. I had twenty minutes simply to tell the truth: "Look what I found, and she's dirty, chipped, and broken like me—like all of us." Every pew was packed tight with parishioners, and one Mass included my wife.

It was the second Mass that touched me the most. I thought that I was dying, bombing. *People hate this. This is not working.* But after I had finished and sat alone, head down, hearing the parishioners leave the church, I looked up to see people on their knees praying before Broken Mary, asking her for help.

"People are praying. Look, Jesus, it's your mom." Watching such prayerful approaches was humbling and powerful.

After each Mass, I had told the congregation that they

could take her with them: "Take her home; take her to hospitals; take her to people who are broken and need her intercession." And they did. Since then, the statue of Broken Mary has been taken by many, traveling to those who need comfort and strength.

These are the thoughts of Father Mark about our friendship and this wonderful development:

> When I first met Kevin Matthews, he was cooking at an auction dinner event. I thought he would be goofy and silly, but he took his cooking very seriously, and prepared an awesome dinner. When he returned to WLAV in Grand Rapids, we reconnected, and I was proud to be on his show every so often. The same personality came through—goofy and silly on air, but serious when he was planning and preparing the show. As we became better friends, and I started to cook with him, the same thread appeared: He liked to have fun, but cooking for the guests required perfection, or close to it, and so no drinking or shenanigans.
>
> I recall the first time Kevin told me about Broken Mary. I thought it was a routine he was developing. When he mentioned the Broken Mary Project, wanting me to be involved, I responded yes, but in the back of my mind I thought very little of it. Wasn't it a gag? During this time, however, Kevin was becoming a regular at weekend Masses, and soon I had him talk to the adult

religious education class about Native American spiri-
tuality. He did a great job. People loved it. I was pleased
that he was attending Mass and getting involved with
the church and school through our cooking and auction dinners. Every so often, he would mention Broken
Mary. Then he asked me where he could get her fixed
up, and I steered him to a place near the church. This led
to more talk of Broken Mary, and I actually saw her at
his home in the corner of his dining room. Still, I didn't
know where this was going, if anywhere.

Kevin invited me to an event at the Franciscan Life
Process Center, in Lowell, Michigan. This was a fund-
raiser for the sisters to whom I had introduced him
months earlier, and he was going to talk about Broken
Mary. I thought the routine must be ready for the public, and I looked forward to hearing his presentation.
He talked about Broken Mary and how he had kept her
broken (though she could have been made like new),
because he was broken. He bared his soul in that room
and shared how his life had changed in all its brokenness, and that God had never deserted him. It was a very
deep spiritual moment for everyone in that room.

On my way back to Grand Rapids, I kept ponder-
ing Kevin's words. I needed him to share his story with
my community at St. Anthony. I knew that many people
could relate, because many of us, if not all, are broken
in one way or another, and we need to keep our faith

in Jesus and Mary, his mother. I asked him the next day if he would be willing to give a reflection about Broken Mary at all of the weekend Masses. He said yes, but he was terrified to speak in church. I had to have several confidence-boosting sessions with him, but I knew he would do a great job.

The day arrived, and Kevin brought the statue of Broken Mary to church. We placed her on a stand near the altar, while he gave a wonderful reflection, just like he had with the Franciscans. I think the people at first thought he was going to do some comedy, but as he shared the story of his brokenness, and related it to Broken Mary and Jesus, people were hooked. After Mass, although Kevin felt he had only done okay and wasn't too pleased, when we turned around, there were five or six women and men kneeling in front of Broken Mary praying! Wow! That is when it all came together.

Broken Mary found a home at St. Anthony of Padua, Grand Rapids, but it was just her resting place. People began to ask to take her to their homes, to the hospitals and nursing homes. Kevin has always said that Broken Mary belongs to everyone and all are welcome to her. He said she likes to travel! The Broken Mary statue remains at St. Anthony, but when she is absent, people know she is out and about bringing comfort to the broken. What a blessing Kevin has been for this parish and for so many broken folks!

Almost immediately, special requests for Broken Mary came to the church. In May, Paulette Lesiewicz's husband brought Broken Mary to her father. Their family had suffered through fifteen years of her mother's Alzheimer's, and then her brother's untimely death, and as her father was failing, they felt broken. Paulette shared what happened:

> It is an amazing blessing to be able to care for and be there when a loved one passes. But it is difficult beyond words. That is why when my husband, Chuck, brought Broken Mary to my father's bedside, a quiet and needed sphere entered that room.
>
> We placed her within [my father's] eyesight and she stayed there for three weeks. We spoke, prayed the Rosary, reminisced, and cried about how very fortunate we were to have had the relationship and love we have had for nearly fifty years. Broken Mary opened that room and only allowed the utmost love to enter. She was an integral part of the process, the ultimate blessing from God, of saying good-bye . . . for now.

Cindy Roberts, who remembers her mother's devotion to Mary, the statue of the Blessed Mother on the family's fireplace mantel, and the lilacs and candles that surrounded her living room rosary altar during May, recalls Mary as a wife, mother, daughter, friend, and woman.

I ask her for intercession daily as I try to carry out these female roles in my life. And when I am broken in my life, I know Broken Mary is right there beside me, encouraging me on my faith journey, because she has had the same kind of struggles. One of my favorite prayers is the Memorare, and I say it daily: "Remember, most gracious Virgin Mary, that never was it known that anyone who fled to your protection, implored your help, or sought your intercession, was left unaided."

Cindy finds great comfort in knowing Mary is praying to her son, Jesus, for her and all her daily struggles. Her hope is to become the woman of faith that Mary is.

"Broken Mary has brought about a new devotion to the Blessed Mother among many of the parishioners of St. Anthony," says Vonnie Clark. "It has been amazing to see the number of people who are relating to the journey of Broken Mary, the broken aspect of our own faith journey, our brokenness. What a blessing to our faith community, where all are welcome, broken and all!"

Lisa Mills, the administrative assistant at St. Anthony of Padua, noticed that "after the parishioners heard the story of Broken Mary, I had many requests for Mary to visit hospitals, nursing homes, hospice facilities, and homes. Many families told me of the peace and comfort she brought to them and their loved ones during their struggles. Mary has taught us all that brokenness can be beautiful."

By the time I was asked to speak at Grand Valley State University, my alma mater, Broken Mary had acquired fifty or more rosaries. It seems that each family who had hosted her at their home had given her a rosary as she left. It had become a custom, and many of the rosaries were very beautiful. The students at Grand Valley were surprised by all of them, but very happy to have Broken Mary with them for an evening. Afterward one student took her home to be with his grandmother, who was very ill.

I have told the story of Broken Mary to many people, in large and small groups. I begin by reminding the audience that this is not about me, and not about a statue; this is about the power of believing in prayer. Many have taken Mary into hospitals, hospice centers, and homes, and they came to this beautiful statue on their own. They simply listened and came to God. What these people said to God, what they asked for, I have no idea, but I do know that they had a personal moment with him. I tell the audiences, "This statue represents all of us, because every one of us is broken, even the pope." I remind them to say the Rosary.

"Whatever is it you are asking for, believe that it will be done, but now you must commit to the Rosary and protecting those not yet born." I always end my presentation simply by saying, "You are loved."

I am certainly not Dr. Phil, and I am no religious scholar. I am not going to tell you what to do or how to live your life, but I do invite you to pray, to give to God, to Jesus, the biggest mess, the worst pile of trash, everything broken about you. Send it off through confession, and free yourself. Believe and then listen to the Holy Spirit. Keep your eyes open and expect something to happen, because you asked; therefore, it shall be done.

Do you believe? Do you love God, Jesus, Mary, and all of those above you? Someday you will see Jesus face-to-face. He may ask you two questions: "Whom have you loved?" and "What have you done for me?" What are you going to say? If you need help with your answer, you might ask Broken Mary.

TWENTY-SIX

The Rosary App

The thought of recording the Broken Mary Rosary never left my mind. I could not help but think, *Why not use my voice to recite the Rosary?* After all, I was a professional broadcaster. What if I could develop my own app that anyone, anywhere in the world could download for free?

In the summer of 2014, I began reading as much as I could about the history of the Rosary, the meaning of each bead, the mysteries, and the honest power of the prayer. Even during war, battles have been won using just the power of prayer through the Rosary. By now, I had the strength and the desire to record the Rosary using my voice, in my studio. How hard could that possibly be?

I soon would find out that I was about to battle nothing human—recording this project, seeing it finally finished, would become a battle between good and evil. My patience and faith would be tested. The voice I heard was no longer saying, *Will you deny me and my mother?* but instead, *Will you fight for me?*

The Rosary has been a mystery to me since, as a child, I watched my mother and grandparents pray with a string of beads, but it was not until my devotion to it during Lent that I learned the respectful power the Rosary contains. When I hold a rosary, I have the entire life of Jesus Christ in my hand, from his nativity to his crucifixion, his ascension into heaven, and his return to earth at the end of time. The power of prayer is so simple and at our fingertips that it should be shared by all.

In 2014 I began recording the Rosary in my studio. I wanted to let the world hear the beauty of prayer through our Blessed Mother Mary. Then I reached out to a dear Chicago friend who designs websites. Edward Silha knew nothing about Broken Mary, so I crossed my fingers and prayed that he would not make fun of me when I told him about the holy journey that had been consuming my life for the past three years. I simply prayed, and without question he agreed to take time out of his busy life to help build a custom free app for the entire world to use.

But what I thought would be a very easy task turned out to be one of the most challenging. *How hard could recording the Rosary be? I have more than thirty years of broadcasting experience and my own recording studio. What could possibly go wrong?*

I had begun writing this book more than a year before, and my priest and dear friend, Father Mark, had encouraged me to journal the mystery of Broken Mary. "People need to know," he said. "People, more than ever, need to pray, and this story is about the broken. We all are broken; we all are starving spiritually." So he had introduced me to a Franciscan, Sister Lucia, who is a writing professor. Interestingly, she lives at the Franciscan Life Process Center, the very place that I had promised the flower shop clerk I would make a donation to.

So we set to work preparing the Rosary. For months I would record the entire Rosary on CDs and send them to Sister Lucia, who would carefully listen to every word I spoke. I soon learned that my diction and articulation were not so good as I had thought.

"Kevin, it's hallowed, not halo."

"Yes, Sister." And back to the studio to do it again.

"You left out a Hail Mary in the second decade of the Sorrowful Mysteries, Kevin."

"Yes, Sister." And back again. Take after take, session after session, months went by. *Am I ever going to get this recorded correctly?* Finally I had a perfect session for the entire Rosary. Now it was time to send it to Chicago via the Internet. But every time I would try to send it, my Internet would crash. I continually tried to update it, but it never reached Chicago. *Why? What is going on?*

I was getting frustrated. Maybe I was not supposed to do this. "God, help me," I prayed, and I asked Sister Lucia, "Why can't I finish this project?"

She laughed. "Good is often opposed by evil," she said. "I'm sure evil hates the Rosary, Kevin. And the Broken Mary app has the potential to be everywhere." Suddenly I felt as if I were in an epic struggle; this was no joke. I was good enough to start the project, and I was going to complete it. I said a prayer: "Jesus, be with me. Let me send this project to Chicago in your name. Let it reach Chicago." And it did.

Ed designed the software that would be submitted to

Apple. Each person who downloaded the app would hear the daily Rosary, be able to select a brief history of Broken Mary, and have the opportunity to send a short prayer. *What could possibly go wrong?*

Every written word was examined again and again by me, Ed, and Sister Lucia, but misspelled words began to appear, extra words I hadn't written. For the next two months the project was stalled due to a series of unusual errors. Finally, after a group prayer, the text was perfect. The Broken Mary app went worldwide, ready to download for free.

"Everyone, look! It works! Look at how beautiful it is!" I shouted. Recently, Ed called to give me the analytics: The Broken Mary app is popular. "Kevin, the most downloads are happening in the Philippines."

That's amazing. Something that began in my basement studio is now being used throughout the world. People old and young, of all nationalities are praying the Rosary, hearing my voice. We are praying together here on earth. The story of Broken Mary is being read by thousands, and thousands are sending personal prayers through this Apple app. That is the power of prayer. Jesus, look at what your mother and the world are doing.

TWENTY-SEVEN

Pilgrim Mary

Remember my wife's brochure that I had with me in the cemetery near Chicago when I was given back the use of my hand and arm? Titled *Our Lady of Fatima: Our Mother Comes to Us*, it tells about the miracle of Fatima in Portugal. In 1917, Our Lady appeared to three small children ages seven, nine, and ten as they were on their way home from tending a flock of sheep. Ultimately, because of the statements of the children, more than seventy thousand people, including newspaper reporters and photographers, gathered at Fatima, where they witnessed the "miracle of the sun" as it rotated like a wheel and changed colors. Today Fatima is a famous pilgrimage destination. The apparition of Our Lady there urged the praying of the Rosary.

Why was this small blue-and-gold Fatima booklet so important to me? When I was diagnosed with MS, I had it with me in my truck. It went with me to treatments and to the cemetery. I had just grabbed anything religious, because I had no rosary, no Bible, nothing except my wife's booklet. I carried it with me to work, kept it on my nightstand at home. It was a spiritual comfort, but most of all, it had an image of the Virgin Mary on the cover.

One early morning in November 2014, I was having a cup of coffee, and I had placed the brochure on the table, but my eyes suddenly saw something I had not noticed before: a web address, pilgrimvirginstatue.com. I could not believe how big it appeared. I took out my iPhone and wrote a simple e-mail to the Pilgrim Virgin Committee in Asbury, New Jersey, whose contact info was given on the website. It went something like this:

> Hello, my name is Kevin Matthews, and I found a statue of the Virgin Mary in a dumpster. I have put her together again, and I would love to come and visit you to see your statue, the famous Pilgrim statue of the Virgin Mary, honoring the miracle of Fatima.

I hit send and off it went. As soon as I sent it, I thought, *If I hear something from these people, I do; if I don't, I don't. God, it is totally up to you.*

That was the first time I had asked God for some kind of sign. *What does all of this mean? Should I be writing a book? Who did I just write to? Jesus, I just wanted to take this statue of your mother out of a dumpster. Look at my life now. What a mess! Show me something, please.*

Each morning after that, I carefully checked my e-mail: nothing from the Pilgrim Virgin Committee. I began to question whether the site still worked. *Who are these people?*

Two weeks went by, when suddenly I saw an e-mail from New Jersey. I opened the e-mail and began to read:

Dear Kevin,

Thank you for your letter. If you are ever in the New Jersey area, we would love to show you the Pilgrim statue of the Virgin Mary.

I immediately wrote back with a very brief description of the Broken Mary statue, telling them that I worked in radio, how much the statue of Broken Mary meant to me, and how others were being touched by its message.

Within one hour I received a phone call. A woman named Joan greeted me. We talked for nearly two hours, and I quickly learned that this group of people are very much active, what the Pilgrim statue is about, and that their group is sanctioned by the Vatican.

Made decades ago, the Pilgrim statue of Mary is the way Mary appeared to Lucia, Francisco, and Jacinta nearly one hundred years ago in Fatima, Portugal. Millions of people have seen the statue, which has been blessed by the pope, and she continues to travel the world, blessing and loving all who see her, all who pray the Rosary, all who simply love her son, Jesus Christ. Importantly, I learned that the one hundredth anniversary of the miracle of Fatima was coming up in just three years, and I was invited to participate. I was speechless. I had only asked for a sign, but I had gotten a big nudge from a very nice author.

Joan Tarca Alix has written *A Gift of Miraculous Visions*, a devotional book of pictures and text. It not only acknowledges the miracle of Fatima, but each page is filled with hope and stories of children and the motherhood of Mary. In celebration of the one hundredth anniversary of Fatima, Alix is publishing a special edition called *A Gift of Miraculous Visions: Fatima—Celebrating Her Centennial.* With a foreword by Catholic speaker Immaculée Ilibagiza, the new edition has additional stories of hope, including a short report on the finding of Broken Mary. Millions will share the beauty of Our Blessed Mother and the miracle of Fatima. You are invited to attend the anniversary in 2017, but you can also begin celebrating the power of prayer, our mother Mary, and the one who loves us forever, her son, our Savior Jesus Christ, right now.

TWENTY-EIGHT

Who Found Whom?

It's been more than four years since I found Broken Mary lying in garbage next to a dumpster. As I write this chapter, I can't help but realize that I did not find the statue by accident, but was guided. Years of prayer led me to her. Nothing is a coincidence, and I am happy that I have learned to listen to my heart.

Today I am in Minnesota, attending a Catholic conference with Father Mark, who blessed the statue three-and-a-half years ago, and who has been such an inspiration and friend during this spiritual adventure. We are smiling at yet another sign of God's grace.

I have never liked flying, and so when our jet was on the tarmac, ready to speed down the runway, pull up into the air, and fly to Minneapolis, I grabbed my iPhone, opened the Broken Mary app, which anyone can download for free, and scrolled down to "Ask for a Prayer." Our jet was waiting to move for takeoff, so all mobile devices were to be turned off, but the prayer requests opened, and I quickly begin typing the shortest prayer possible: "Mary, Jesus, bless this flight and make us land safely in Minneapolis, and please tell my guardian angel to help me this week." I hit send and turned off my phone as the jet moved onto the runway and up, higher and higher into the air. For years, whenever I fly, I gently knock on the window frame and pray a simple prayer my Iroquois grandfather taught me: "To all my relations, to the sky world, I come into your world. Bless me and protect me. Thank you." The captain informed us that the ride would be very bumpy because of storms building ahead of us. *Great. I knew I should have turned off my phone sooner.*

The flight was smooth and Father Mark had arranged for a wheelchair and attendant to meet us at the gate. (My legs have been weak lately and my balance is poor; plus this is a huge airport.) Pushing me in the wheelchair, Father Mark walked at a fast pace, zipping past people, and I thought we were going to collide with other travelers. *Wow, was that close!* We passed store after store, a bar, and gift shops. I thought people were looking at me and thinking, *He's not crippled; he's a fat ass.*

Father Mark noticed an ATM and suggested we get some cash. I reached into my back pocket and pulled out my wallet. With the money and a long white receipt tucked into my pants pocket, we left the secured area, a point of no return without a ticket, and finally arrived at the baggage claim area. Father Mark grabbed his bag and mine, but when I checked my wallet, the ATM card was not there.

"I don't have my card," I said, rummaging through my pockets and my wallet. "I must have left it at the ATM." Only passengers with tickets were allowed back in the secured area.

"Would Kevin Matthews please pick up a white security phone and call Security, please. Would a Kevin Matthews please pick up a white security phone and call Security, please," we heard the airport page announce at that very moment.

"They must have my ATM card." We began backtracking in the direction of the ATM, but were soon stopped by a large red sign: SECURE AREA. MUST HAVE TICKET TO ENTER. We rushed toward an information attendant. I told her my name and that I had just been paged. She smiled and called Security.

"Yes, I have a traveler here by the name of Kevin Matthews and you just paged him."

She pulled the phone away from her ear and said, "They have your ATM card." This dear woman made arrangements to meet the security agent and rescue my card. As she left, Father Mark and I smiled.

"I've got a great guardian angel this trip." We were both laughing, because this airport is so big, if my ATM card had been stolen, or if I could not have found it, our trip would have been ruined. The prayer on the Broken Mary app had essentially been "Protect this flight and send me a great guardian angel, please." The attendant was handing me my green ATM card.

"Thank you so much," I said.

She smiled and replied, "Have a great week."

The power of prayer, and more important, the power and friendship of Jesus Christ, our big brother, is always with us, holding our hand tightly, even in a large and crowded airport. Truly believing in God day by day without question, trusting Jesus, acknowledging his mother, and remembering those who have left the earth takes faith.

"Ask and you shall receive." How have these little mysteries made you the person you are today? Believe that you are never alone, and most of all, that you are loved, even in a crowded airport.

TWENTY-NINE

I Love Radio

The reason I decided to write the story of Broken Mary is simple: I wanted to acknowledge the miracles I have witnessed during my life, thanking God for each, and to leave my family and fans the real story. I have experienced terminations, format changes, and personal challenges throughout my radio career, but these hardships have been few, occurring between the good times, the milestones, which by far surpass the sadness I have endured. I was a radio voice in Chicago for seventeen years running, producing groundbreaking programs with the highest ratings, as well as historic promotions and events.

Here I sit, in my home office with walls that are covered with framed pictures of me and my peers, of my producer, Doc, at the first ever "Beat Kev's Meat BBQ" in 1993. I can see newspaper sections: BEST MORNING RADIO—KEVIN MATTHEWS from the *Chicago Tribune* readers poll, FAVORITE RADIO PERSONALITY IN CHICAGO, KEVIN MATTHEWS from the *Chicago Sun-Times*, and FAVORITE MID-DAY SHOW—KEVIN MATTHEWS. There are paintings of Jim Shorts and photos of former radio personalities I have worked with, including Steve and Gary, Jonathon Brandmeier, and Wolfman Jack. To my left is a photo of Jimmy DeCastro, my first boss, the guy who hired me from St. Louis; and one of Larry Wert, my favorite boss and friend of all, who has the most photos on my wall.

Trophies on the desk behind me include Father of the Year, Showtime's Funniest Person, Billboard awards, Radio and Records awards, and one of my proudest awards, the Top 25 Personalities of the Past 25 Years in Radio. They have piled up throughout the years, but it's never been about the awards; it's always been about the audience, the Kevheads, my fans, whom I dearly love. I owe everything to them.

Kevheads are young and old, first, second, and now third generation. They are male and female, doctors, cops, professional athletes, drug addicts, priests, military, judges, Native Americans, Asians, Muslims, drunks in Dublin, the handicapped, midgets, and sisters. In the thirty years since I first opened a microphone, Kevheads have come and gone. Some of them I have known personally. Their responses have generated the synergy of my career that began in the Midwest of America and has stretched via the Internet to cover the globe. Radio has blessed me. God has blessed me, and I thank him, Our Blessed Mother, and my Kevheads each and every morning. But recently my gratitude was rounded by a certain disease.

THIRTY

It's Just Beginning

While attending church at St. Anthony's, I felt suddenly lost. Normally, I can see the statue of Broken Mary standing next to the main altar, which for years has been her place, because I usually sit in the very front pew, partly because I no longer want to hide in the back of the church as I did for decades. I enjoy sitting where I can see her smile, her gentle eyes looking up, her neck holding so many beautiful rosaries.

But she was not there because of construction. In the face of so many troubles in the world and in our Church, St. Anthony's has new hope in the form of construction inside and out, a major expansion to accommodate our ever-growing congregation. And during the rough work phase, the statue had been placed in the rectory, protected from the construction dust and workers.

There will be a new chapel, and Broken Mary will be there when she is not on a mission. The public will continue to take her with them into hospitals, hospices, schools, and homes, but now she will also witness marriages and baptisms inside this holy chapel. What a wonderful thing! Just four years ago, she was ready to be thrown away.

While sitting in my pew, I heard Father Mark say to the congregation, "People from around the world will come to see our new church," and it was then that I thought, *And will read the story of Broken Mary.*

As Mass ended, I was standing next to Father Mark, silently watching him say good-bye to his parishioners, and I was worrying that people might forget about Broken Mary, that they would no longer need to take her into hospitals and homes.

Just then a young boy of about nine came up to Father Mark with his grandmother. He tugged at the priest's chasuble, asking, "Father Mark, where is Broken Mary? We want to take her home, because my grandmother wants to pray. Me, too."

Father Mark turned to me. "Yes, she is in the back. Kevin will help you put her into your car to take her home."

I turned to Father Mark and said, "And a little child will lead them."

What happens to Broken Mary is no longer something I worry about. She never belonged to me. I was blessed to find her, and I give thanks for that every day. She has changed my life. I am confident that those who need her and her son, Jesus, will be able to find her.

DECISION
point

THE DYNAMIC CATHOLIC
CONFIRMATION EXPERIENCE

*"I am convinced this is the best invitation
to young Catholics to accept and live their faith
that I have encountered."*

— CARDINAL DONALD WUERL, Archbishop of Washington

REQUEST YOUR FREE* PROGRAM PACK
at DynamicCatholic.com/Confirmation

*The complimentary program pack includes:
the complete DVD series containing 72 short films,
the student workbook, and the leader guide.*

*Just pay shipping.

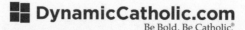

THE
DYNAMIC CATHOLIC
INSTITUTE

[MISSION]

To re-energize the Catholic Church in America by
developing world-class resources that inspire people to
rediscover the genius of Catholicism.

[VISION]

To be the innovative leader in the New Evangelization
helping Catholics and their parishes become
the-best-version-of-themselves

Join us in re-energizing the Catholic Church.
Become a Dynamic Catholic Ambassador today!

DynamicCatholic.com
Be Bold. Be Catholic.®